The Bible declares that where there is no vision the people perish. A vision can be a dream, and a dream can be a vision. In order to bring a vision/dream into reality, there must be a dreamer, a visionary if you would. Charles Blake is without question a dreamer and a visionary. I have known Charles for more than sixteen years, both as a minister of the Gospel and as a very personal friend. Because of his impeccable integrity, scholarship, leadership, and personal commitment to the things of God, I believe him to be eminently qualified to challenge Christians everywhere to dream big.

Dr. Fredrick K. C. Price

It is with a deep spiritual respect for my good friend, Bishop Charles Blake, who is a pastor's pastor—one uniquely raised up by God with an incredible ministry of integrity, power, and tremendous depth of relevance to the body of Christ—that I wholeheartedly recommend *Free to Dream* to all believers who dare to dream God's dream and see God's vision. For forty-three years, my beloved co-laborer, Bishop Blake, has exemplified what it means to give birth to God's dream and God's vision through his impeccable life, his powerful ministry, and his exemplary commitment as husband, father, friend, and pastor.

Morris Cerullo, President
Morris Cerullo World Evangelism

Bishop Charles Blake has been a source of inspiration and encouragement to young pastors across this country for years—not only through his powerful and penetrating sermons, but through his evident example! He has the heart of a shepherd and the humility of a sheep. He has not chosen to simply accept what has always been but to dream of what might be and then work and pray to bring it to pass. I am certain that you will be challenged to dream as you engage in this book of possibility and prophecy, *Free to Dream.*

Pastor Marvin L. Winans

In reflection, I know of no other person of the Church world who is more qualified to write about successful dreams than Bishop Charles E. Blake. Someone asked, "How do dreams come true?" The answer, "One must wake up and do something about that which was dreamed." Obvious and simple as it may seem, this question oftentimes goes unanswered. Shattered and unfulfilled dreams are the result. But this man is a successful dreamer, one who not only *answered* the question but has *become* the answer. I am delighted that he is kind enough to share the manifestation of those successful dreams with us. Truly, we are *Free to Dream.*

Bishop Paul S. Morton
Greater Saint Stephen, F.G.B.C.

CHARLES E. BLAKE Sr.

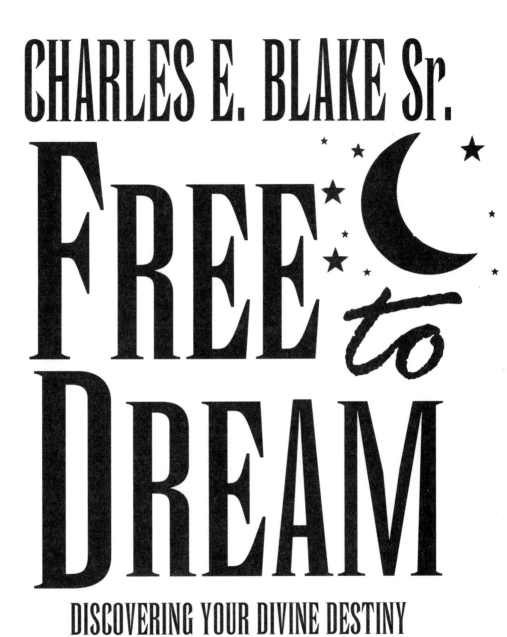

FREE *to* DREAM

DISCOVERING YOUR DIVINE DESTINY

ALBURY PUBLISHING
Tulsa, Oklahoma

Free to Dream
Discovering Your Divine Destiny
ISBN 1-57778-183-X
Copyright © 2000 by Bishop Charles E. Blake Sr.
West Angeles Church of God in Christ
3045 S. Crenshaw Boulevard
Los Angeles, California 90016

Published by ALBURY PUBLISHING
P. O. Box 470406
Tulsa, Oklahoma 74147-0406

Table of Contents

Dedication

This book is dedicated to
my darling wife, Mae, who works
as hard to bring my dreams to pass as I do.

Introduction

Thirty years ago I sat on the thirteenth floor of a building on the campus of what was then the Garden Grove Community Church, pastored by Dr. Robert Schuller. As I gazed across the city of Los Angeles from that magnificent church and looked at all God had done through Dr. Schuller, I cried, "Lord, can't You do something through me?" God had given me a dream too, and as I sat and pondered, the dream in my mind and spirit expanded. I became all the more convinced that I had to do whatever it took in order to accomplish something great for the kingdom of God.

Over the next thirty years, my dream came true and grew in ways I never expected. Along the way, of course, I endured afflictions I never foresaw and shouldered burdens I thought would break me. Yet now I am blessed to shepherd West Angeles Church of God in Christ, one of the fastest-growing churches in America. We have a membership of more than 17,000. Our eighty ministries reach out to the community with the love of Jesus Christ. We provide low-cost housing, feed hungry people, minister to prisoners, give free counseling, and in many other ways help meet the community's needs.

As I've struggled to reach my God-given dreams, I've seen parallels between the Christian walk and the life of Joseph. We all dream, and we all encounter affliction, yet many Christians never achieve their dreams. That's why I am writing this book: to bring Joseph's struggle to life in a way that will help you attain your God-given dreams.

God gave Joseph powerful dreams, but his was a journey of peaks and valleys, of rapid ascents and landslide descents. Although he was his father's favorite, his brothers hated him with a passion. They left him for dead, but he was rescued. Then he was sold into slavery, but he was raised to a responsible position in his master's house. He was unjustly accused of a terrible crime and thrown into prison only to become the head trustee in charge of his fellow prisoners. He helped a member of Pharaoh's staff gain his freedom, but the "grateful" employee forgot Joseph and left him to languish in prison for another two years. Finally, he used his God-given ability to interpret a dream for Pharaoh, who gave him charge over all the land of Egypt. What a breathtaking, roller-coaster ride of a life!

Joseph's dreams did not come true until after he had become a great ruler in Egypt, however. Finally, the day came when his brothers did indeed come and bow down to him, and he was able to save his family from famine—which was God's true intention all along. But how did Joseph survive all those hardships to achieve his God-given dream? How can we?

As you read this, I urge you to look into the very face of God and say, "God, I will give my everything to make the dream You have given me a reality. If You have done great things through others, then I believe You can do something great through me."

It is my prayer that God will reveal His wonderful plan for your life as you read this book. I pray that you will rise up and commit yourself to transform your world through the power of the Almighty, that you will receive a vision from God, and that you will strive to make your God-given vision a reality. I pray that this is the place, this is the time, and you are that person.

Commit yourself to the vision God has given you, and He will bring it to pass—beyond your wildest dreams!

We Are Called to Dreams

Chapter 1

Fifty-six years ago in the black South African homeland of Transkei, Thabo Mbeki was born into a nation ravaged by the terrible monster of apartheid. His life was filled with danger and suspense because his parents were dedicated members of the African National Congress. They risked their lives to bring freedom and justice to their country.

Through his early years, young Thabo was imbued with the dream of freedom. By the time he was nine years old, his parents were so active in the ANC that their arrest by South African security forces was eminent. As a result, they sent Thabo away to live with an uncle. At the age of ten he presented himself to the ANC, declaring he was ready to go to jail to help accomplish the dream of freedom for his people. They told him to come back when he was older.

Thabo continued to pursue his dream head-on. By the age of seventeen, he had become a leader in the ANC Youth League and was expelled from school for leading a student strike against racism. Then, at the age of twenty, his dream took a different turn. He and twenty-seven other young students were called into a secret meeting with ANC pioneer Nelson Mandela. Mandela had been hiding from the South African government to avoid arrest as he led the fight against racism. In this secret meeting, Mandela stood before them in disguise and assured them that the struggle against apartheid would one day be over. He reminded them that when the dream of freedom was fulfilled, leaders would be needed to bring about reconstruction and governance. These hand-picked students, he announced, were to be smuggled out of South Africa so that they might be educated and trained for the day when they would rule the country.

Thabo Mbeki was sent to England, far from family and friends. Mandela went to prison, but the dream he shared in 1964 sustained Mbeki during the twenty-eight-year exile that followed. For all those years, he dreamed and contemplated the vision of freedom for South Africa and leadership for himself. He studied, he prepared, and he maintained his commitment to freedom and the ANC.

Finally, in his late forties, Mbeki returned to South Africa. He soon was designated by the ANC to handle some of the very first and most sensitive negotiations with the white minority regime. It is said that he had become a masterful negotiator. A short time later, he was so involved in the administration of the new president, Nelson Mandela, that he was called the "de facto" prime minister by many. He became deputy president of South Africa in 1994. In 1997 he replaced Nelson Mandela as the head of the ANC, and in June, 1999, the people of South Africa elected him president, the successor of Nelson Mandela.

Was it an easy road? In the thirty-five years since the dream was imparted to Mbeki, his father was jailed, his son and a nephew were killed, and his life was frequently in danger. Yet he studied and prepared, and finally the dream came to pass. Were we to ask him what it was that sustained him during all those years of struggle, he would say, "I always kept the dream before me—the dream of freedom for my people."

Standing Firm

The story of Thabo Mbeki also reminds me of the biblical story of Joseph. Like Mbeki, Joseph eventually saw his God-given dreams come true, but he went through terrible times on the way. Between his days in his father's house and his days in the Pharaoh's house, Joseph spent years in turmoil and pain. He was beaten, enslaved, imprisoned, maligned, and forgotten on his way to the fulfillment of his dream. How did Joseph survive to achieve his God-given dream?

- He established a close relationship with God. Nothing can happen without that foundation.

- He gave God's Word and His Law top priority in his life.

- He continually sought God's heart in every matter.

- He refused to compromise under pressure but persisted in righteousness.

- He never surrendered to hopelessness.

- He never took his eyes off the dream.

Understanding the story of Joseph can help you make your God-given dream a reality. You may know God has a wonderful plan for your life, but somewhere along the way, your dreams have been squashed, diverted, damaged, disrupted, and lost.

You've lost sight of what God wants to do with you. You may even feel that you can never reconnect with God's plan.

Far too many of us have allowed the world's agenda to rule us rather than following God's best plan for our lives. We've given in to the dream killers and the dream stealers. We've come to see the troubles inflicted on us as barriers impossible to break through and have lost sight of our dreams. We've despaired over the length of time it's taken to reach our God-given dreams. We've settled for far less than God's best.

But I believe that God's plan for our lives is inevitable and irresistible. What He starts He'll finish. We simply have to discern His vision for our lives and work wholeheartedly toward those goals. Simple, yes, but not easy. That's why the ups and downs in the life of Joseph are so instructive to us. As we study his life, notice that not only does he go through afflictions, but God uses those very afflictions to propel him into the fulfillment of his dreams. This is why we must not give up on our lives! No matter what we've been through, we may be right on the edge of reaching our God-given dreams without realizing it. On the day his dream came true, Joseph had breakfast in the dungeon and ate dinner in the palace!

Make It Real

Before we talk about reaching for our dreams, we need to define what dreams are not. First, they aren't wishes. "Gee, I wish I had a million dollars." A wish is a passing fancy, an idle thought, or a whim without consequence or impact. A wish carries no weight and packs no punch. It's spoken and gone in a second.

Wishes pass
with the moment.
Dreams carry the
weight of eternity.

A wish is simply a desire without the application of any prayer or effort. Some people have a wishbone where their backbone should be! To live a significant life, to do God's will, we need to stop the mindless wishing that things would somehow be different. People say, "I wish God would work in my life," but they don't make the effort to study His Word or pray to seek His will. They say, "I wish my kids wouldn't run wild," but they don't firmly and consistently discipline those children, raising them up in the nurture and admonition of the Lord.

Dreams are real. They are not whimsical wishes, nor are they fantasies. A dream without a godly goal and a righteous plan of action is a fantasy. I see the strength of fantasies in the eyes of folk lining up to buy lottery tickets. Whenever the prize reaches unusually big numbers, you see regular folk — hard-working and usually sensible folk — succumb to lotto fever. In every community you can hear the cry of families going hungry because the grocery money went to buy lottery tickets. That's not a God-given dream! That's just greedy fantasy.

What's worse, we have Christian fantasies too! I know of folk who say they want to be missionaries to Timbuktu, yet they won't tell their next-door neighbor about the power of God. Others say they desire to have great Christian ministries, but they won't teach fourth graders in Sunday school.

Unlike wishes and fantasies, God-given dreams are the visions that guide our lives and propel us to do what God has called us to do. If you truly have a God-given dream like Joseph, you will go anywhere and do anything to stay in obedience to God's will whether it feels good or not. Joseph didn't expect to wind up in a pit, in slavery, or in prison when he dreamed the dream God gave him, yet he trusted God's plan through it all.

I'm often asked, "Do we all have God-given dreams?" Absolutely! The prophet Joel proclaims that this is the dispensation of dreams and visions. He announces that dreamers are coming:

> *And it shall come to pass afterward, that I will pour out my spirit upon all flesh; and your sons and your daughters shall prophesy, your old men shall dream dreams, your young men shall see visions:*
>
> *And also upon the servants and upon the handmaids in those days will I pour out my spirit.*

Joel 2:28-29 KJV

Joel proclaims that Spirit-filled men and women are to be the primary repositories of God's dreams and visions. If you are filled with the Holy Ghost, you ought to have a dream! The apostle Peter confirms this when he speaks of the outpouring of the Holy Ghost on the early church at the Day of Pentecost:

> *But this is that which was spoken by the prophet Joel.*

Acts 2:16 KJV

Why is there an outpouring now, at the end times? Jesus gave the answer in Acts 1:8:

> *"But you shall receive power when the Holy Spirit has come upon you; and you shall be witnesses to Me in Jerusalem, and in all Judea and Samaria, and to the end of the earth."*

Obviously, when you receive a God-given dream, not a wish or a fantasy, God will give you the strength and courage to walk it out, just like He did Joseph. When your dream is real, God will supernaturally bring it to pass in your life.

People Are Perishing

Joel proclaims that we are living in the time of great dreams and godly dreamers, but why? What are the dreams for? We know that the Almighty does nothing without purpose. I believe the answer is found by just looking around us and seeing the world through God's eyes. Hear the world through God's ears, and you will be changed forever.

At this time more than any other, we need an "ends of the earth" vision. Proverbs 29:18 KJV says: **Where there is no vision, the people perish.** People are perishing without visions, and many of these people are very close to us. An epidemic of violence plagues our cities. Angry, hopeless, frustrated young men and women are robbing, killing, and being killed themselves. The harvest of centuries of slavery and discrimination has now grown up to terrorize us. The drug abuse epidemic contributes to the flood of robbing and killing, while the drugs themselves directly kill many and make many "dead" even while they live. There is no vision, no dream, and so the people perish.

- Sexual immorality is directly responsible for the AIDS epidemic, which is killing hundreds of thousands of men and women. They have no godly vision, so they perish in sexual perversion.

In a vision,
God allows us to
see what He sees.

- Marriages are perishing. Without the godly vision of how to serve as the husbands and wives of today and tomorrow, couples are handicapped, disabled, and divorced.

- Teenage girls who have no godly vision for their lives, no understanding of their inherent worth and priceless value to a God who loves them, become mothers while they are still children—just to prove they can do something creative.

- In thousands of cities, towns, and villages in the world, people are perishing for lack of food when there is more than enough food in the world to feed them. No one has the vision from God to feed them!

- War, tyranny, and revolution cause the blood of those who are perishing to flow in the streets of the world. No one has the vision from God to bring peace to the war-torn nations!

- Disease, ignorance, and poverty cause many to perish on every continent on this earth of ours. No one has the vision from God to meet the needs with His power and grace!

People are perishing because they lack godly vision or because a vision has not been communicated to them and accepted by them. People who have no vision lie, steal, and destroy. People who have no vision die. People who have no vision commit suicide. People who have no vision have no reason to keep on working and believing.

Because people are perishing, God is raising up dreamers!

What Is a Dream?

A vision or a God-given dream is the revelation of God's will and plan for our lives. In a vision, God allows us to see what He sees. He reveals to us what He wishes us to know and do. We do not have the answer to life's riddles within ourselves. There are many things which we cannot know except by divine revelation. We cannot save the perishing in our own thinking or under-standing. We must get a vision from God, or we could end up at the wrong place at the wrong time doing the wrong thing and perishing ourselves.

> *There is a way which seemeth right unto a man, but the*
> *end thereof are the ways of death.*
>
> Proverbs 14:12 KJV

> *But the natural man does not receive the things of the*
> *Spirit of God, for they are foolishness to him; nor can he know*
> *them, because they are spiritually discerned.*
>
> 1 Corinthians 2:14

A vision is a picture of what God wants to bring to pass and what we must do to implement His plan. Vision is spiritual discernment. Those most likely to do God's work are those who are most sensitive to His heart. Those who have vision are those who can discern His plans for the future and work toward them.

I stand to announce that God is ready for some great and mighty dreams and accomplishments! All we need to do is ask Him.

*"Call to Me, and I will answer you, and show you great
and mighty things, which you do not know."*

Jeremiah 33:3

Let us think some great thoughts, by faith see some great
visions, then walk in faith toward what we have seen. A dream
given by God is inevitable and irresistible. God never gives a
dream for which He does not assume responsibility, that He does
not bring to pass. He always starts with a dream, and if He starts
it, be assured that He will finish it. If God causes you to will it,
He will help you to do it.

*Being confident of this very thing, that He who has begun
a good work in you will complete it until the day of Jesus Christ.*

Philippians 1:6

When I read the story of Joseph and use a little imagination, I
can see Joseph riding in the second most beautiful chariot in the
kingdom of Egypt pulled by six beautiful white horses. People
are bowing to him and speaking well of him. I see his brothers
who tried to kill him now bowing low before him. He is dressed
in exquisite and fashionable apparel. I see him approaching his
beautifully furnished mansion on the hill, where his breathtak-
ingly attractive wife who has been given to him awaits his
return. As he prepares to enter the door, I ask him, "Joseph, how
did all this happen?"

Joseph smiles and answers, "It all started with a dream."

Child of God, I see you in the future, and you look much
better than you look right now! I see you going higher. I see you

meditating on the vision God has given you. I see you fulfilling the wonderful dream God has for your life. And there is no end to the blessings that He has for you—now and forever!

Walking *With* God

Chapter 2

Now Israel loved Joseph more than all his children, because he was the son of his old age. Also he made him a tunic of many colors.

But when his brothers saw that their father loved him more than all his brothers, they hated him and could not speak peaceably to him.

Now Joseph had a dream, and he told it to his brothers; and they hated him even more. . . .

Now when they saw him afar off, even before he came near them, they conspired against him to kill him.

Then they said to one another, "Look, this dreamer is coming!

"Come therefore, let us now kill him and cast him into some pit; and we shall say, 'Some wild beast has devoured him.' We shall see what will become of his dreams!"

Genesis 37:3-5,18-20

As badly as he started out, why didn't Joseph wind up in a mental institution instead of the Pharaoh's palace? Why did he attain his God-given dreams rather than accept defeat and give up on life? With his background, Joseph had every reason to have emotional problems. Jacob, his father, had children by four different women. His mother, Rachel, died early in his life. His father played favorites, and this might have caused Joseph, the favorite son, to become a spoiled brat. It certainly caused his brothers to hate him. His father even dressed Joseph oddly. He was given a coat of many colors that set him apart from his older brothers.

Not surprisingly, Joseph experienced terrible jealousy and animosity in his home. What was worse, his parents were extremely old when he was born and were unable to protect him from his brothers, who hated him to the point of violence. The Bible says that they hated him and could not speak peaceably to him (Genesis 37:4). Throughout his youth, he probably never heard a kind or positive word from them. This hatred must have increased dramatically after he announced that he had repeatedly dreamed of them bowing down to him.

Now Joseph had a dream, and he told it to his brothers; and they hated him even more.

So he said to them, "Please hear this dream which I have dreamed:

"There we were, binding sheaves in the field. Then behold, my sheaf arose and also stood upright; and indeed your sheaves stood all around and bowed down to my sheaf."

And his brothers said to him, "Shall you indeed reign over us? Or shall you indeed have dominion over us?" So they hated him even more for his dreams and for his words.

Then he dreamed still another dream and told it to his brothers, and said, "Look, I have dreamed another dream. And

*this time, the sun, the moon, and the eleven stars bowed down
to me."*

*So he told it to his father and his brothers; and his father
rebuked him and said to him, "What is this dream that you
have dreamed? Shall your mother and I and your brothers
indeed come to bow down to the earth before you?"*

*And his brothers envied him, but his father kept the matter
in mind.*

Genesis 37:5-11

By the time Joseph was seventeen, his big brothers hated him
so much that as soon as they saw the opportunity, they decided
to kill him. They even informed him of their intentions before-
hand. They threw him into a deep pit to let him die a slow death
by thirst and exposure. After seeing a caravan of Ishmaelite
traders nearby, however, they decided it would be more
profitable to sell their little brother into slavery instead.

The terrible treatment at the hands of his own flesh and
blood should have been enough to drive him over the edge, yet
Joseph survived and even thrived. How? Even in his youth and
immaturity, *Joseph walked with God and he never quit believing in —
and working toward — his God-given dream.*

When Joseph became a slave in the house of Potiphar, an
officer in the army of Egypt, he could have seen his enslavement
as the end of his dream and just quit trying. He could have
become the most useless servant in Potiphar's household,
suitable for only the most menial chores. But Joseph kept his
eyes on the dream and continued to walk with the Lord. He

served Potiphar to the best of his God-given ability, and God blessed that effort with great success.

> *The LORD was with Joseph, and he was a successful man; and he was in the house of his master the Egyptian.*
>
> *And his master saw that the LORD was with him and that the LORD made all he did to prosper in his hand.*
>
> *So Joseph found favor in his sight, and served him. Then he made him overseer of his house, and all that he had he put under his authority.*
>
> *So it was, from the time that he had made him overseer of his house and all that he had, that the LORD blessed the Egyptian's house for Joseph's sake; and the blessing of the LORD was on all that he had in the house and in the field.*
>
> *Thus he left all that he had in Joseph's hand, and he did not know what he had except for the bread which he ate.*

Genesis 39:2-6

If the Lord was with Joseph, it follows that Joseph was with the Lord. What did it mean to "be with the Lord"? It meant that Joseph sought the Lord continually. It meant that he considered his relationship with the Lord to be the most important in his life. It meant that he was a man of prayer and absolute spiritual commitment. When others were reaching for the things of this world, Joseph was reaching for the higher things of God. Psalm 119:164-167 expresses the relationship Joseph maintained with God:

> *Seven times a day I praise You,*
> *Because of Your righteous judgments.*

Great peace have those who love Your law,
And nothing causes them to stumble.

LORD, I hope for Your salvation,
And I do Your commandments.

My soul keeps Your testimonies,
And I love them exceedingly.

The fruit of Joseph's excellent service soon elevated him to a place of trust and responsibility. He was put in charge of Potiphar's entire household. Potiphar entrusted Joseph with the stewardship of all he possessed, knowing that he would use his God-given abilities to make his master's estate prosper. Potiphar soon learned that it wasn't even necessary to check Joseph's figures when he did the books because he was scrupulously honest.

Dealing With Disappointment

At this point, Joseph must have felt that his dream would soon come to pass. He'd come a long way from being his brothers' punching bag, a long way from dying in a pit. He'd bounced back from his setbacks and was on his way to achieving his dream. Walking with God was paying off!

Then along came Potiphar's wife.

Now Joseph was handsome in form and appearance.

And it came to pass after these things that his master's wife cast longing eyes on Joseph, and she said, "Lie with me."

When others were
reaching for the things
of this world, Joseph
was reaching for the
higher things of God.

> *But he refused and said to his master's wife, "Look, my*
> *master does not know what is with me in the house, and he has*
> *committed all that he has to my hand.*
>
> *"There is no one greater in this house than I, nor has he*
> *kept back anything from me but you, because you are his wife.*
> *How then can I do this great wickedness, and sin against God?"*
>
> *So it was, as she spoke to Joseph day by day, that he did*
> *not heed her, to lie with her or to be with her.*
>
> Genesis 39:6-10

Surely Joseph must have known what kind of woman he was dealing with. He probably knew he'd have trouble when he rejected her propositions. He may have known it would even mean the loss of his job. It certainly would have been easy for him to simply give in to her repeated demands. A lesser man would have. But Joseph chose to do the right thing. For a man who walked with God, it didn't require any thought at all. Not only was she another man's wife, but his master had trusted him to be with her. He would neither commit adultery nor betray his master's trust for a moment of pleasure. He turned her down repeatedly. He not only rejected her advances, but eventually he literally ran from her grasp.

The reaction of Potiphar's wife to Joseph's rejection of her was predictable. She tried to destroy him. She accused him of attempting to rape her and he was thrown in jail. Can you imagine the crushing blow this was to Joseph? After he had made the best of being enslaved and had worked his way up to a position of great trust in his master's household, just when it looked like he was on track for his God-given dream to come true, suddenly the bottom fell out and he was thrown into prison.

Disaster struck, but Joseph continued to walk with God. He didn't give up on his God-given dream. Even in prison, he continued to make the best of his situation, knowing that what God had showed him would ultimately come to pass.

> *But the LORD was with Joseph and showed him mercy, and He gave him favor in the sight of the keeper of the prison.*
>
> *And the keeper of the prison committed to Joseph's hand all the prisoners who were in the prison; whatever they did there, it was his doing.*
>
> *The keeper of the prison did not look into anything that was under Joseph's authority, because the LORD was with him; and whatever he did, the LORD made it prosper.*

Genesis 39:21-23

Once again, Joseph could have given up and surrendered to the dream killers. He could have gotten mad at God for dropping the ball on the dream he'd been following so faithfully for so long. But Joseph walked with God and kept faith in the dream no matter what his circumstances were. He made the best of the situation and God caused him to prosper. Even in prison, he was appointed steward over the other prisoners!

Darkest Before Deliverance

While he was running the prison, there were two inmates who were from Pharaoh's palace, a butler and a baker. Joseph was asked to seek God for the meaning of a vision Pharaoh's butler had received. Based on the dream, Joseph prophesied that the butler would be released from prison and restored to his place of honor in Pharaoh's household. When the butler was indeed released, Joseph must have thought he had a chance of being freed because he now had a friend in Pharaoh's palace. His hopes, however, were dashed when the butler forgot Joseph for two long years.

Joseph continued to languish in prison until Pharaoh himself had a dream no one could understand. When none of Pharaoh's magicians could interpret the dream, his butler remembered Joseph's ability to interpret dreams and told Pharaoh about him. Pharaoh sent for Joseph.

Pharaoh had dreamed of seven fat cows coming out of the river, then seven skinny cows coming and eating the fat cows. He had a second dream in which plump heads of grain were devoured by seven thin heads. None of his magicians or wise men could understand that these dreams meant a famine would come upon Egypt and God was warning them to prepare for the famine by storing food.

> *And Pharaoh said to Joseph, "I have had a dream, and there is no one who can interpret it. But I have heard it said of you that you can understand a dream, to interpret it."*
>
> *So Joseph answered Pharaoh, saying, "It is not in me; God will give Pharaoh an answer of peace."*
>
> Genesis 41:15-16

Giving God the proper credit, Joseph interpreted the dream.

We may not control
what happens to us, but
we can always determine
what our reaction to
adversity will be.

"God has shown Pharaoh what He is about to do.

"Indeed seven years of great plenty will come throughout all the land of Egypt;

"but after them seven years of famine will arise, and all the plenty will be forgotten in the land of Egypt; and the famine will deplete the land."

Genesis 41:28-30

From the dreams, Joseph suggested a strategy whereby Pharaoh could sustain the people of Egypt and greatly enhance his own position. He suggested that Pharaoh appoint a discerning and wise man to oversee the collection of one-fifth of all the grain produced during each of the years of plenty. This chosen man would further arrange to store the surplus grain throughout the kingdom as a reserve for the seven years of famine. He would then distribute the grain to those in need.

Pharaoh realized that he had just such a wise man in front of him.

So the advice was good in the eyes of Pharaoh and in the eyes of all his servants.

And Pharoah said to his servants, "Can we find such a one as this, a man in whom is the Spirit of God?"

Then Pharaoh said to Joseph, "Inasmuch as God has shown you all this, there is no one as discerning and wise as you.

"You shall be over my house, and all my people shall be ruled according to your word; only in regard to the throne will I be greater than you."

And Pharaoh said to Joseph, "See, I have set you over all the land of Egypt."

Genesis 41:37-41

Divine Satisfaction

Things were looking up for Joseph more than ever before. He was beginning to see the realization of his God-given dream. As second in the kingdom only to Pharaoh, he was responsible for storing up vast amounts of grain during the seven years of good harvests. Then, during the years of famine, Pharaoh put him in charge of food sales and distribution.

Meanwhile, back in Canaan, famine also struck. After two years of poor harvests, Joseph's father, his brothers, and their families had run out of food. Jacob sent his sons—Joseph's abusive big brothers—to Egypt because he had heard that there was an abundance of food there.

When they arrived in Egypt, Joseph's brothers were brought before the chief of food distribution in hopes of buying enough grain for their family to survive. They were probably scared. They may have heard that this young ruler was second only to Pharaoh himself, and if he didn't sell them grain, they would starve.

And Joseph's brothers came and bowed down before him with their faces to the earth.

Joseph saw his brothers and recognized them, but he acted as a stranger to them and spoke roughly to them. Then he said

to them, "Where do you come from?" And they said, "From
the land of Canaan to buy food."

So Joseph recognized his brothers, but they did not recog-
nize him.

Genesis 42:6-8

Well, there they were. His big brothers—the guys who had
thrown him into a pit to die and sold him as a slave—were on
their knees with their faces in the dirt. Although he didn't make
it easy on them, finally Joseph revealed his identity, forgave
them, gave them food, and saved the lives of his entire family.

And Joseph said to his brothers, "Please come near to me."
So they came near. Then he said: "I am Joseph your brother,
whom you sold into Egypt.

"But now, do not therefore be grieved or angry with
yourselves because you sold me here; for God sent me before
you to preserve life.

"For these two years the famine has been in the land, and
there are still five years in which there will be neither plowing
nor harvesting.

"And God sent me before you to preserve a posterity for
you in the earth, and to save your lives by a great deliverance.

"So now it was not you who sent me here, but God; and
He has made me a father to Pharaoh, and lord of all his house,
and a ruler throughout all the land of Egypt."

Genesis 45:4-8

Joseph had finally seen his dream come true. His brothers and father had finally come and bowed down to him as he had dreamed years before. But the journey from pit to palace would have killed a lesser man. Until Pharaoh brought him out of prison and put him in charge of his kingdom, Joseph's life was the kind of stuff which makes for nervous breakdowns! What made the difference? He kept his focus on God! In the end, Joseph's personal verdict was, "What you guys meant for evil, my God has turned to all our good." (See Genesis 50:20.)

Staying Focused

Without God, people have committed suicide under less severe circumstances. Joseph came from a dysfunctional and incomplete family, the kind that usually produces dysfunctional, incomplete individuals. But Joseph did not become dysfunctional. He did not commit suicide. He did not roll up into an emotional fetal position and resign from life. How did Joseph retain his sanity? How did Joseph survive all these wild ups and downs?

Joseph had a secret. *No matter what happened or how he felt, he kept on walking with God toward his dream.* When he was hated, when he was stripped, when he was in the pit, he kept his eyes on God. When he was sold into slavery, when he was lied about, when he was a prisoner in jail, he kept on seeing the vision. He kept on seeing it in his heart until he saw it come to pass. He kept on reaching for it until he grabbed hold of it with his hand.

Joseph survived because he did not allow people to make him bitter. He only allowed them to make him *better*. His brothers made him better. Potiphar's wife made him better. Pharaoh's chief butler made him better. We may not control what happens to us, but we can always determine what our *reaction* to adversity will be. We must let adversity make us better. The United States Marine Corps has a saying about that: "Whatever doesn't kill me makes me stronger!"

Paul described this godly reaction to times of adversity thousands of years later in his letter to the church at Philippi:

> *For I have learned in whatever state I am, to be content:*
>
> *I know how to be abased, and I know how to abound . . . I have learned both to be full and to be hungry, both to abound and to suffer need.*
>
> *I can do all things through Christ who strengthens me.*
>
> Philippians 4:11-13

Both Joseph and Paul knew what we must learn: In the walk of faith, it is vital to keep our eyes on the dream and our focus on the goal, rather than on our circumstances. Long-distance wilderness hikers have learned to set their course by a distant mountain peak rather than focus on their immediate surroundings. If they take their eyes off their goal, they'll get distracted and wind up wandering in circles. To reach our goals we must do the same: focus our eyes and our hearts on our God-given dreams rather than on the stumps and thorn bushes that we encounter on our way.

As You Do Unto Others . . .

Another reason Joseph not only survived but thrived in adversity was that he worked to help the dreams of others come to pass. He didn't just advance toward his own goals. With a servant's heart, he worked on other folks' dreams. For example, Joseph worked on Potiphar's dream. He said, "Potiphar, I have been unjustly enslaved, but while I'm here in your house, I'll work to my utmost to make your vision for this house come to pass. What is your vision for this house?" And what happened? God blessed all Joseph did.

He said to the jailer, "I shouldn't be in your jail, but while I'm here I'll work as hard as I can to make your vision for this jail come to pass." Again, God blessed all that Joseph did.

He said to the butler and the baker in prison, "I'm going to work on your dreams so that they might come to pass." And God blessed him with the interpretation of their dreams.

He worked on Pharaoh's dreams. He interpreted the dreams of seven fat years and seven lean years so that Pharaoh was able to prepare and save his kingdom. And again, God blessed all that Joseph did.

It's not surprising that as he worked on everybody else's dreams, his own dream came true. Your dream will not come true until you make somebody else's dream or vision come true. Church members ought to go to their pastor and discern what vision the Lord has given to him for the church so that they can work wholeheartedly toward that vision. It's true here and now just as it was with Joseph: When you help to bring to pass God's vision for someone else, God will make your dreams come true.

> *Why do you say, O Jacob,*
> *And speak, O Israel:*
> *"My way is hidden from the* LORD,
> *And my just claim is passed over by my God"?*

> *Have you not known?*
> *Have you not heard?*
> *The everlasting God, the* LORD,
> *The Creator of the ends of the earth,*
> *Neither faints nor is weary.*
> *His understanding is unsearchable.*

> *He gives power to the weak,*
> *And to those who have no might He increases strength.*

> *Even the youths shall faint and be weary,*
> *And the young men shall utterly fall,*

> *But those who wait on the* LORD
> *Shall renew their strength;*
> *They shall mount up with wings like eagles,*
> *They shall run and not be weary,*
> *They shall walk and not faint.*

> Isaiah 40:27-31

Ultimately, God blessed *us* through Joseph. His entire life of trials and victories was designed by God to preserve the lineage of the family of Jacob, out of which would come the Messiah, Jesus. In Genesis 45:7, Joseph told his brothers:

And God sent me before you to preserve a posterity for you in the earth, and to save your lives by a great deliverance.

Joseph's tenacity in following his God-given dream saved his family from famine. This was a vital part of God's plan of our redemption because King David was descended from Judah, Joseph's brother, and Jesus was descended from King David.

Joseph survived his crazy roller-coaster life because he had patience, endurance, and faith in his God-given dream. For thirteen years he faced one terrible trial after another, one adversity after another. But Joseph never surrendered to hopelessness. He never gave up. Child of God, don't you give up either!

Shake It Off and Step On Up!

Joseph's survival as an abused child of a dysfunctional family reminds me of a story my father used to tell. A farmer had an old mule that was too old to work and consumed more food than the farmer was willing to give. The farmer decided to get rid of him by pushing the old mule down into a dry well and burying him there. And so he did.

For days the farmer would come and throw all kinds of debris down the well on top of the old mule. The trash would hit the mule and hurt him, but when the farmer wasn't looking, the mule would shake the trash off his back, step on the trash, and move up a little higher.

After doing this each day for several days, the farmer was confident that he had buried the old mule. He threw one last massive load of rocks, automobile fenders, and old tires down the well. All of this hit the old mule and hurt him, but he shook it off and stepped on top of it. By this time he had shaken off so much trash and had stepped up so much that he was able to climb out of the well and walk to the stream and pasture for cool water and nourishing grass. He might well have said to the farmer, "You tried to bury me, but I used everything you threw at me to climb higher to freedom."

Child of God, that's what we must do to follow the dreams God has given us! We can rise above our failures and our defeats. We can rise above abuse. We can rise above addictions. We can rise above dysfunction. We can rise above guilt. When adversity comes, we just shake it off and step on up! Shake it off and step on up! Sure it hurts us, but each time we shake it off and step on up, we get that much closer to achieving our God-given dreams!

Seeking *God's* Heart

Chapter 3

Twenty-five years ago, Chuck Colson was on top of the world. A powerful man with a glamorous position, he served as special counsel to the president of the United States. A few months later, however, he was headed to prison. As he entered a federal penitentiary with other shackled prisoners, Colson thought to himself, *I always thought I'd contribute more with my life, but that dream is over. Now I'm nothing but a convicted felon.*

Most Christians know the rest of the story. Chuck Colson had received Jesus Christ as his Lord and Savior just before he went to prison, and while he was there, God placed a new hope and dream in his heart. After serving time in prison for his Watergate-related offense, Colson became convinced of the need for a ministry devoted to sharing the Good News of Jesus Christ with men and women in prison. Upon his release he founded Prison Fellowship Ministries, which has ministered to thousands of prisoners, ex-offenders, and their families in the years following.

Colson's greatest defeat—being sent to prison—was the beginning of God's greatest use of his life. Although he couldn't see it at the time, it was not until his own dreams came crashing down around him that God was able to instill a new, divine set of dreams in their place. In the same way, we can overcome our past defeats and failures, even now, to reach for God-given dreams far beyond anything we've imagined.

Not All Josephs

We're not all Josephs in this world. We haven't all followed God-given dreams since our youth, nor have we all trusted God to attain them through thick and thin. In fact, some of us think we can no longer be used by God because of what we've done. We're damaged goods, too tarnished and too tainted to be of any use to God. We may even be as bad as that Old Testament leader who used his God-given authority to seduce a married woman and then arrange for her husband to be killed in battle. What would God say about a man like that? The Bible says that he was "a man after God's own heart"! (See 1 Samuel 13:14.)

Was God being unjust or having selective amnesia? No! The crucial point here is that both David and Saul were imperfect and flawed individuals. Both of them sinned against God, but only one of them repented. God named David king of Israel to replace the disobedient King Saul.

> And Samuel said to Saul, "You have done foolishly. You have not kept the commandment of the LORD your God, which He commanded you. For now the LORD would have established your kingdom over Israel forever.
>
> "But now your kingdom shall not continue. The LORD has sought for Himself a man after His own heart, and the LORD

*has commanded him to be commander over His people, because
you have not kept what the LORD commanded you."*

1 Samuel 13:13-14

*And when He had removed him [Saul], He raised up for
them David as king, to whom also He gave testimony and said,
"I have found David the son of Jesse, a man after My own
heart, who will do all My will."*

Acts 13:22

I have been enthralled and fascinated by this verse for many
years. It seems to me that the man described as "a man after
God's own heart" would certainly be capable of attaining his
God-given dreams. It also seems that this man would be a good
model for those who wish to walk with God in all they do. But
David was a rotten sinner compared to our boy Joseph. How is
he a role model for the rest of us dreamers?

Dealing With Sin

The secret to being a person after God's own heart, capable
of reaching our God-given dreams, lies in comparing David not
with Joseph, but with Saul. Specifically, *how David and Saul dealt
with sin in their lives determined the degree to which they walked with
God and attained the dreams He gave them.*

What happens when we are confronted with evidence of sin
in our lives? We can either harden our hearts and continue in sin,
or we can repent and turn from our sins. We can either line up
with God's standard of holiness or ignore God and go our own

way. No matter what David did, he ultimately realized his sin and repented. Saul never did.

Look at the story of King Saul's downfall in 1 Samuel 15. God sent Saul specific commands through the prophet Samuel. Saul was instructed to gather his army and attack Amalek. He was to totally destroy everything that breathed—every man, woman, child, and animal. Saul didn't refuse Samuel's God-given instructions, but he didn't follow them to the letter, either. He gathered his army and attacked Amalek, killing thousands of men, women, and children. However, trusting his own judgment, he spared the Amalekite king to take home as a trophy and kept a few of the best sheep, lambs, and oxen so the people could sacrifice them to the Lord.

If we didn't know what the prophet had told Saul, we might think he was a godly king. "See there, he sacrifices only the best to the Lord!" But after this campaign, God spoke to Samuel:

> "I greatly regret that I have set up Saul as king, for he has turned back from following Me, and has not performed My commandments."

> 1 Samuel 15:11

Here's where the difference between David and Saul becomes obvious. The prophet Samuel went to confront Saul. When the king saw Samuel, he greeted him proudly:

> "Blessed are you of the LORD! I have performed the commandment of the LORD."

> 1 Samuel 15:13

"Oh really?" Samuel said. "Then why do I hear sheep bleating and cattle lowing?" That's why God regretted appointing Saul king. Saul showed that walking with God was not his highest priority by exhibiting selective obedience. He twisted God's instructions to fit his own agenda and pleasure.

Saul might have saved his crown by promptly and sincerely repenting, but instead he argued with Samuel. Ultimately, Saul only went through the motions of repenting so that Samuel would walk at his side on the way back to Jerusalem, which would make everybody think things were fine between God and Saul. He cared more about what his people thought of him than what God thought of him.

In a minute, we are going to see that David dealt with his sin in a very different manner than Saul did. God knew Saul's heart, that he was not a man after His heart. He rejected him as king because he disobeyed and never truly repented. Thus, by understanding what Saul did wrong, we can see the qualities that make up a man after God's own heart.

Where Saul Went Wrong

First, Saul was no longer "little in his own eyes." (See 1 Samuel 15:17.) In fact, Saul began to think he was pretty hot stuff. We should not feel inferior to anyone else, but neither should we feel that we are wiser than God or better than others. Truly great people are naturally magnanimous and treat others with respect because they render *God* the awe and respect He is so richly due.

Second, Saul was unwilling to operate according to God's schedule. He did not trust God and considered his own ways better than God's ways. He used God's specific directions as general guidelines instead of absolute commands, trusting in his own wisdom as his guide.

Third, Saul placed material goods above obedience to God's direct instructions. To impress his people, he disobeyed God's Word.

Where else did Saul go wrong? During his reign over Israel, he also turned to evil, devilish powers for guidance and assistance. He sought to foil, frustrate, and impede God's plan for His chosen king. He tried to kill what God had blessed. And after all this, Saul never changed or even gave evidence of a sincere interest in repentance.

Saul's heart condition resembled that of the children of Israel generations before:

> *The Holy Spirit warns us to listen to him, to be careful to hear his voice today and not let our hearts become set against him, as the people of Israel did.*
>
> *They steeled themselves against his love and complained against him in the desert while he was testing them.*
>
> *But God was patient with them forty years, though they tried his patience sorely; he kept right on doing his mighty miracles for them to see.*
>
> *"But," God says, "I was very angry with them, for their hearts were always looking somewhere else instead of up to me, and they never found the paths I wanted them to follow."*

Hebrews 3:7-10 TLB

It was not until his own dreams came crashing down around him that God was able to instill a new, divine set of dreams in their place.

Those are the characteristics that disqualified Saul from being a person after God's own heart. We should desire to be like David rather than Saul, to be a person after God's heart.

People who seek God's heart are blessed.

People who seek God's heart are elevated.

People who seek God's heart are anointed.

People who seek God's heart prosper.

People who seek God's heart are protected.

People who seek God's heart are identified with God so that when someone messes with them, they mess with God himself.

An Inside Job

Abraham Lincoln was ugly, skinny as a rail, and had an irritating hillbilly accent, yet he was one of America's greatest leaders. His character exhibited a heart for God and his fellow-man. Experts say that Lincoln couldn't get elected now because he would look and sound so bad on television. That's probably true. We have a natural tendency to look on the outside when choosing leaders. We're more likely to choose those who are smooth and good-looking, who carry themselves like a leader. And you have to admit, we've elected ourselves some sorry leaders that way! They look good and sound good on television, but their hearts are turned toward money, power, and privilege rather than serving the people.

The Bible reveals that the primary factor in God's selection of David was not visible, physical, or even behavioral. It was

internal. God saw something He liked in David's heart. When
He sent Samuel to Jesse's house to anoint the new king of Israel,
Samuel thought for sure one of the oldest and strongest of
Jesse's sons would be chosen. Instead, God chose the "runt of
the litter," a little shepherd boy who seemed very rough around
the edges! God instructed Samuel with these words:

> But the LORD said to Samuel, "Do not look at his appear-
> ance or at his physical stature, because I have refused him. For
> the LORD does not see as man sees; for man looks at the
> outward appearance, but the LORD looks at the heart."

1 Samuel 16:7

After God saw David as a man after His own heart, he was
on a fast track to success. God started putting him on people's
hearts. When Saul needed an anointed musician to bring peace
to his disturbed spirit, someone recommended David. And
David was a great blessing to Saul. God's anointing upon
David's praise and worship calmed the troubled king.

David was the only one who had the courage to fight Goliath
because he was the only one to realize he was fighting with the
power of God, not his own power. After that, Saul chose him to
be the leader of his armies.

> So David went out wherever Saul sent him, and behaved
> wisely. And Saul set him over the men of war, and he was
> accepted in the sight of all the people and also in the sight of
> Saul's servants.

1 Samuel 18:5

The problem was, David became popular with the people, even more popular than Saul. When Saul heard people singing David's praises, he became jealous and did everything he could to kill him, but the Lord protected David.

> *"For the* LORD *your God is He who goes with you, to fight for you against your enemies, to save you."*

> Deuteronomy 20:4

The Lord did all this for David because he sought God's heart, and he became Israel's greatest warrior and king. Being a man after God's own heart caused David to prosper, and although he was rich, he was generous with his riches. In fact, he gave a single building-fund gift equivalent to $100,695,000 for the new temple. Don't you wish you had a David in *your* church? I do!

> *Therefore David blessed the* LORD
> *before all the assembly; and David said:*
> *"Blessed are You,* LORD *God of Israel,*
> *our Father, forever and ever.*

> *"Yours, O* LORD, *is the greatness,*
> *The power and the glory,*
> *The victory and the majesty;*
> *For all that is in heaven and in earth is Yours;*
> *Yours is the kingdom, O* LORD,
> *And You are exalted as head over all.*

> *"Both riches and honor come from You,*
> *And You reign over all.*
> *In Your hand is power and might;*

Truly great people are
naturally magnanimous and
treat others with respect
because they render God
the awe and respect
He is so richly due.

In Your hand it is to make great
And to give strength to all.

"Now therefore, our God,
We thank You
And praise Your glorious name.

"But who am I, and who are my people,
That we should be able to offer so willingly as this?
For all things come from You,
And of Your own we have given You."

1 Chronicles 29:10-14

God saw to it that David's descendants ruled Israel for many generations. And then God arranged things so that Jesus was called a son of David, because David was in the messianic lineage. All this proves that God does special things for a person after His own heart. For that very reason each of us should want to be a person after God's own heart; plus, seeking the heart of God will also release His dreams in our lives.

Taking Full Responsibility

When He chose David, God looked on the heart because He could see that David would always return to Him. As a person after God's own heart, David knew how to repent. In Psalm 51:10 David wrote,

Create in me a clean heart, O God,
And renew a steadfast spirit within me.

There are many who would say, "How could David be a person after God's own heart when he committed adultery with Bathsheba and had her husband killed?" Make no mistake, it was an evil and disgraceful thing David did, but he bore the consequences. The first child born of that sinful union died. David and his family suffered for years to come because of his sin, and during the time he was in sin, he was certainly not a man after God's own heart. It was the greatest failure of an otherwise spectacular life. But after he came to his senses, David looked at what he'd done through the eyes of God and was horrified. He repented with fear and trembling, knowing that he was at the mercy of a holy and righteous God.

> *Have mercy upon me, O God,*
> *According to Your lovingkindness;*
> *According to the multitude of Your tender mercies,*
> *Blot out my transgressions.*
>
> *Wash me thoroughly from my iniquity,*
> *And cleanse me from my sin.*
>
> *For I acknowledge my transgressions,*
> *And my sin is always before me.*
>
> *Against You, You only, have I sinned,*
> *And done this evil in Your sight —*
> *That You may be found just when You speak,*
> *And blameless when You judge.*

Psalm 51:1-4

When he realized how he'd sinned against God, David didn't fool around. He knew how to repent and was quick to do so:

The sacrifices of God are a broken spirit,
A broken and a contrite heart —
These, O God, You will not despise.

Psalm 51:17

Could David have done better following after God? Sure he could have, just as we all can. David should have repented of his first stray thought when he saw Bathsheba. He didn't have to take that lustful thought to the next step, nor did he have to take action on those thoughts. At several points along the way, he chose to sin and not to repent. People who are most successful in realizing their God-given dreams keep their accounts short with God. They catch sin in its earliest stages and repent quickly to nip it in the bud. This prevents the enemy and their flesh from hindering their progress in fulfilling the call of God.

Notice the contrast between David and Saul. Saul did all he could to dodge taking responsibility for his sin, and when that did not work, he tried to make things right with Samuel for appearance sake. Saul never even went to God. On the other hand, when the prophet Nathan confronted David about his sin, he didn't try to rationalize, explain, wiggle out, or pass the blame. He went straight to God, confessed, and repented. By contrast, when some people apologize, you almost wish they would save themselves the trouble. There's no repentance in their apology. They might be sorry they were *caught*, but they're not sorry they *did wrong*. So they say, "Well, if you think I'm wrong. . . ." or "That really wasn't my fault, but if you think it was. . . ." Then they look for someone else to blame.

"That's just how my mama raised me."

"Now look what you made me do!"

They dig up excuses.

"I certainly don't think Scripture applies to us here and now."

"I would go to church, but that's my only day off."

People after God's heart, mature Christians, shouldn't make excuses when caught in sin. Kids learn it naturally. When we were kids, most of us were caught with our hands in the cookie jar at one time or another. We'd deny doing anything wrong, even with a mouth full of crumbs. Then when that didn't work, our backup plan was to blame little brother or sister. It was probably hard for our parents to keep from laughing as we tried to avoid taking the rap for what we'd so obviously done.

Well, ducking responsibility was cute when we were two or three, but when we're thirty or forty, it's pitiful. A key step in walking with God and being a person after God's own heart is taking responsibility for our actions. It's facing the fact that *we* are responsible for what we do, for who we are, for our failures as well as our successes, for our flaws as well as our strengths. To walk with God, to be people after God's heart, to reach our God-given dreams, we have to accept responsibility for our sins.

If we say that we have no sin, we deceive ourselves, and the truth is not in us.

If we confess our sins, He is faithful and just to forgive us our sins and to cleanse us from all unrighteousness.

If we say that we have not sinned, we make Him a liar, and His word is not in us.

My little children, these things I write to you, so that you may not sin. And if anyone sins, we have an Advocate with the Father, Jesus Christ the righteous.

And He Himself is the propitiation for our sins, and not for ours only but also for the whole world.

1 John 1:8-10; 2:1-2

This passage of Scripture provides us with the proper way of dealing with our hearts when we, like David, wander away from God. We must examine ourselves and face up to the hard truth of our sin. We should ask God to reveal the sin we don't see, then we must apply 1 John 1:9 to any sin He uncovers.

The Bible describes a believer's renewed and regenerated heart as a heart inclined toward God, a heart strengthened and enlightened by God. A believer's heart should render obedience to God. It should be a heart filled with faith, trust, love, fear of God, fidelity, and zeal. It should constantly seek God, be joyful, upright, clean, pure, sincere, repentant, devout, wise, tender, holy, compassionate, and lowly.

Seek His Heart in Praise

Another reason David was a man after God's own heart was because he worshipped and praised God. He wrote scores of psalms of praise, the words which churches still sing today. Whenever God significantly dealt with him, from saving his skin to rebuking his sin, David wrote a psalm to express what was happening in his walk with God. He spent much of his life putting the inexpressible glories of God into words and music.

I will bless the LORD at all times;
His praise shall continually be in my mouth.

My soul shall make its boast in the LORD;
The humble shall hear of it and be glad.

Oh, magnify the LORD with me,
And let us exalt His name together.

I sought the LORD, and He heard me,
And delivered me from all my fears.

Psalm 34:1-4

As king, I'm sure David acted in a regal manner when conducting his royal affairs; but when he praised the Lord, he wasn't afraid to cut loose and *praise!* Once he shouted and danced before the Lord with such reckless abandon that his wife was completely embarrassed. (See 2 Samuel 6:16.) That didn't slow him down, though. He kept on shouting praises and dancing even after his wife got mad. David knew it was good to be a fool for God! He was never shy about praising Him and dancing unto the Lord.

My heart is steadfast, O God, my heart is steadfast;
I will sing and give praise.

Awake, my glory!
Awake, lute and harp!
I will awaken the dawn.

I will praise You, O LORD, among the peoples;
I will sing to You among the nations.

For Your mercy reaches unto the heavens,
And Your truth unto the clouds.

Be exalted, O God, above the heavens;
Let Your glory be above all the earth.

Psalm 57:7-11

Many folk today will scream themselves hoarse at a basketball game or hoot and holler at a comedian's jokes, but they won't exert themselves a bit to praise God. Why do we get more excited over something that has no eternal value to us? Why don't we get more fired up about the One who saved us from our sins and allows us to become sons of God? Why don't we get beside ourselves when we realize God places dreams of the impossible inside us and then gives us His wisdom and ability to see them realized? These are things to get excited about!

More than that, we are *commanded* to give God great praise.

Give unto the LORD, O you mighty ones,
Give unto the LORD glory and strength.

Give unto the LORD the glory due to His name;
Worship the LORD in the beauty of holiness.

Psalm 29:1-2

Praise the LORD!
Praise God in His sanctuary;
Praise Him in His mighty firmament!

Praise Him for His mighty acts;
Praise Him according to His excellent greatness!

Praise Him with the sound of the trumpet;
Praise Him with the lute and harp!

Praise Him with the timbrel and dance;
Praise Him with stringed instruments and flutes!

Praise Him with loud cymbals;
Praise Him with clashing cymbals!

Let everything that has breath praise the LORD!
Praise the LORD!

Psalm 150:1-6

Our praise expresses our love and respect for God. Our praise expresses our faith in Him and His promises, and without faith it is impossible to please God. (See Hebrews 11:6.) Praise includes thanksgiving, and praise brings God close in a very special way, for the Lord inhabits the praises of His people. (See Psalm 22:3.) David was someone who knew these things and made them part of his everyday life. Is there any wonder that God did great and mighty things through David?

A Flawless Role Model

Although there are many things about David's life we should imitate, he was flawed. Every human being who has ever lived and will live is flawed except one. God provided a perfect model for us in Jesus of Nazareth, the son of David. He is the one to follow.

For to this you were called, because Christ also suffered for us, leaving us an example, that you should follow His steps.

1 Peter 2:21

Although we should all have God-given dreams, certainly we're not all Josephs, nor are we even Davids. We're unique individuals. But when we think we can no longer be used by God because of our failures and our weaknesses, we're wrong. Why? Because neither Joseph nor David followed the Lord entirely in their own strength and wisdom but through the power and guidance of the Holy Spirit. Even with all our liabilities, God is still working in us to bring the dreams He's given us to fruition. We just have to cooperate.

> *Therefore we also, since we are surrounded by so great a cloud of witnesses, let us lay aside every weight, and the sin which so easily ensnares us, and let us run with endurance the race that is set before us,*
>
> *looking unto Jesus, the author and finisher of our faith, who for the joy that was set before Him endured the cross, despising the shame, and has sat down at the right hand of the throne of God.*

Hebrews 12:1-2

Remember, all of that old life was covered by the blood of Jesus when we became new creations in Christ. That old sin should have no power over us to keep us from reaching our dreams. We must not allow Satan, the accuser of the brethren, to lie to us and tell us our old lives disqualify us from being used by God in His kingdom.

> *Therefore, if anyone is in Christ, he is a new creation; old things have passed away; behold, all things have become new.*

2 Corinthians 5:17

Remember too that subsequent sins—even the ones we commit today—are gone forever as soon as we repent and confess them. If we are quick to repent, we can maintain our close walk with the Lord. This is why God gave us 1 John 1:9! So deal promptly with sin, follow hard after God, and seek His face in everything. Pray with a listening ear. Read God's Word as if you were on the Titanic and the Bible held directions to an empty lifeboat! Be a person who steadfastly seeks after God's own heart, and He will see that you attain the dreams He gives you.

Against *the* Flow

Chapter 4

I beseech you therefore, brethren, by the mercies of God,
that you present your bodies a living sacrifice, holy, acceptable
to God, which is your reasonable service.

And do not be conformed to this world, but be transformed
by the renewing of your mind, that you may prove what is that
good and acceptable and perfect will of God.

Romans 12:1-2

Idries Shah, in his *Tales of the Dervishes,* tells this fascinating story. It seems that a prophet predicted that all the water in the world, except that which had been stored and hidden away, would disappear. After a short time, new water would appear which would make men insane and cause them to behave altogether differently when they drank it.

Most people ignored the prophet and his prophecy, but one man immediately began hiding large quantities of water in a remote location. Sure enough, after awhile all the water disappeared. This man went to his hiding place and remained there, drinking his water. Soon the new waters returned to the earth, but this man continued to drink his own water.

When he began to associate with people who had begun drinking the new water, he found them totally mad and irrational. Unfortunately, all of them thought him to be totally mad and irrational. They would show him only rejection, hostility, or pity, but never acceptance and understanding. After many days he found the pain of his isolation to be so great that he decided to drink the new water and become mad, even though he had an ample supply of saved water. Being different and rejected was so unbearable, he was willing to sacrifice his sanity in order to be accepted.

Dreamers Are Different

As Joseph pursued his God-given dream, he must have felt that the rest of the world had gone mad. Nobody understood him. Nobody accepted him. His brothers wanted to make a memory of him, the Ishmaelite traders wanted to make a slave of him, and Potiphar's wife wanted to turn him into her boy-toy. But all he wanted to do was to fulfill the dream God had given him. No one but God would accept Joseph just as he was.

How tragic it is that there are millions of people who are willing to act crazy just so they can feel accepted. And I say *feel* accepted because most people are incapable of extending real acceptance. They are so busy trying to prop up their own egos and to deal with their own inner conflicts and relational deficiencies, all they care about is themselves, never anyone else. Acceptance is something you can give only when you have received it.

I shall never forget a little lame duck I saw in a park in Monterey, California. She was in a pond with a flock of ducks who abused her. They pecked her to chase her away. But every time the flock would move, she would move with them. She continued to receive more of the same treatment. I wanted to yell to her, "Leave them! They're not feeding you or protecting you. They're abusing you." But off she went with them, as if to say, "I'd rather be with them, despised and abused, than to be alone."

As we go through life, and especially during our developmental years, we have many needs. Three of them are the need to be accepted, the need to feel acceptable (or worthy of acceptance), and the need to feel capable or competent. These needs cannot be met in isolation; others must be involved. When they are not met, our emotional development and maturity can be affected, sometimes to the point of neurosis or psychosis. As children of God, however, we are never alone. If not one human being affirms us and tells us of our inherent value and worth, our Father God will. This is probably one of the greatest advantages and joys of being a Christian.

When we have God-given dreams like Joseph, those dreams may run against the grain of what is acceptable to our friends and family, but God will give us all the support and strength we need if we turn to Him. Joseph told his big brothers about his dream of them bowing down to him. I guess he thought they would encourage him to reach for that dream, to follow it wherever it took him. Instead, they responded by conspiring to kill him. Soon Joseph learned that he could only depend on God! Everyone else was against him and would let him down.

Even Jesus had this need. In the Garden of Gethsemane, He was praying just before His arrest and crucifixion, and He wanted Peter, James, and John to stay awake and pray with Him. He expected them to do just that because for three years He had done everything He could for them. But when He needed them for one hour, they let Him down. At this critical hour, they dropped the ball. They weren't even concerned enough to stay awake. But when they let Him down, He relied all the more on God His Father. When people let you down, turn your disappointment into a stepping-stone to a closer walk with God.

Folks will often let you down as you follow your God-given dream, so I would like to suggest a wonderful way to approach life. See the world as a vast mental institution. Imagine that we are on the staff of that institution and the rest of the world are the inmates. From this perspective, we'll seldom be surprised by what people do—after all, they're crazy! We take a logical, clinical, and therapeutic approach to dealing with them, and we won't be shocked or offended at anything they do. I can just visualize myself as a psychiatrist looking at a raging patient in a mental institution and saying, "Hmm, how interesting." I'm not surprised at all. We expect people to do strange things in a mental institution, and if we don't expect people to do strange things in the world, we're in for a rude awakening!

God Defines Us

Most people approach this whole matter of acceptance and belonging in the wrong way. The priority is usually to get the world to think favorably toward us, which is why we're all

having identity crises! We simply don't know who we are because we are allowing outside influences to define us. If we continue to redefine ourselves to please others, we'll never figure out who we really are, and if we have no firm concept of ourselves, we'll spend our lives being less than we could have been. We'll never attain our dreams.

Proverbs 23:7 says that whatever we think in our heart is what we are. Our thinking defines us. One of the definitions of "define" is "to fix or mark the limits of."[1] When we define ourselves, we determine our boundaries in life. We are nailing down our character, our personality, our standards, and our belief of what is right and what is wrong.

We've heard the fable of the eagle who hatched among chickens and thought he was a chicken until he heard the calls of eagles and redefined himself. We've heard the fable of the swan who was born among ducks and thought he was an ugly duckling until he saw a beautiful swan who told him, "You are one of us, and you shall become like us." The little swan redefined himself.

> *He came to His own, and His own did not receive Him.*
>
> *But as many as received Him, to them He gave the right* [KJV says, "power"] *to become children of God, to those who believe in His name.*
>
> John 1:11-12

---

[1] *Merriam-Webster's Collegiate Dictionary,* Tenth Edition (Springfield, MA: Merriam-Webster, Incorporated, 1996), p. 303.

When people let you
down, turn your
disappointment into
a stepping-stone to a
closer walk with God.

When we receive Jesus as our Lord and Savior, we receive the right and the power to become all God created us to be. What we *have been* does not have to dictate what we *must be* in the future. What we *are now* is not our definition of what we *will be* tomorrow. It's time for us to redefine ourselves according to what God thinks of us, not according to what that crazy world thinks. Here is a verse where God tells us exactly what He thinks about us:

> *For I know the thoughts that I think toward you, says the* LORD*, thoughts of peace and not of evil, to give you a future and a hope.*
>
> Jeremiah 29:11

With promises from God like Jeremiah 29:11, we should be constantly growing and developing into more and more mature Christians, advancing toward the attainment of our God-given dreams. Myles Munroe said, "To know the nature of a thing, ask the maker of that thing. Let the maker of the thing, who knows the true nature, capacity, and ability of that thing, define that thing." Since God is our Maker, only God should define us. No one has the right or authority to define you but God himself. The devil owns and controls the unsaved but not the saved, so the devil can't define us, nor can his people. Any other definition but God's is invalid. We should never listen to Satan, the accuser of the brethren, when he tries to define us. We must realize that if the devil can get us to accept his lying definition of us, he can keep us from attaining our God-given dreams—which means he derails God's plans.

What God Really Thinks of Us

Let's go to the Word of God to get some insights into God and His right to define us. We might be surprised to find what God truly thinks of us.

> *Know that the LORD, He is God;*
> *It is He who has made us, and not we ourselves;*
> *We are His people and the sheep of His pasture.*

Psalm 100:3

> *O LORD, You have searched me and known me.*
>
> *You know my sitting down and my rising up;*
> *You understand my thought afar off.*
>
> *You comprehend my path and my lying down,*
> *And are acquainted with all my ways.*
>
> *For there is not a word on my tongue,*
> *But behold, O LORD, You know it altogether.*
>
> *You have hedged me behind and before,*
> *And laid Your hand upon me. . . .*
>
> *Where can I go from Your Spirit?*
> *Or where can I flee from Your presence?*
>
> *If I ascend into heaven, You are there;*
> *If I make my bed in hell, behold, You are there. . . .*
>
> *For You formed my inward parts;*
> *You covered me in my mother's womb. . . .*

My frame was not hidden from You,
When I was made in secret,
And skillfully wrought in the lowest parts of the earth.

Your eyes saw my substance, being yet unformed.
And in Your book they all were written,
The days fashioned for me,
When as yet there were none of them.

Psalm 139:1-5,7-8,13,15-16

Before we took the stage, the curtain lifted, and the story was told, God had already written the script from the beginning to the ending. All we have to do is play our roles. God writes our history before we live it. If we follow the script, He will bring His plans and our dreams to pass. The chaos we see in people's lives comes when they improvise their lines and refuse to follow the script. When that happens, the drama turns into a tragedy.

"Remember the former things of old,
For I am God, and there is no other;
I am God, and there is none like Me,

"Declaring the end from the beginning,
And from ancient times things that are not yet done,
Saying, 'My counsel shall stand,
And I will do all My pleasure.'

". . . Indeed I have spoken it;
I will also bring it to pass.
I have purposed it;
I will also do it."

Isaiah 46:9-11

Have you ever watched a good movie that you've seen before, but no one else in the room has? Only you know the hero gets the girl and it all turns out great in the end, but everyone else has to see how it comes out. Well, God knows the end of the movie. He sees the end of our lives here on earth from the beginning. He is our Maker, our Owner, our Controller, our Source. It is in Him that we live, move, and have our being. We can accomplish our dreams only to the degree that we believe this and act on that belief.

Along with who we are and where we're going, we need to know with whom we are to go. This especially applies to those who are looking for mates. It would be foolish for us to commit to someone based on the fact that we both happen to be at the same place now, if both of us don't know where the other intends to go in the future. That reminds me of the saying, "Yes, we're lost, but we're making great time!" A Christian must find a mate whose dreams are compatible with their own, so that when they arrive, they'll be appropriate company. To arrive at the destination of our God-given dreams, we cannot associate with just anybody. We can't have close fellowship with everybody. We must choose our mate and our friends according to God's guidance. God's definition of us determines what kind of friends we have.

When we begin to allow God to define us, it is very important to understand that He is our loving Father. He loved us so much that He gave His Son Jesus to die for our sins. The Bible says He loves us with an everlasting love (Jeremiah 31:3) and promises in Romans 8:32 that **He who did not spare His own**

We must realize that
if the devil can get us
to accept his lying definition
of us, he can keep us from
attaining our God-given
dreams——which means
he derails God's plans.

Son, but delivered Him up for us all, how shall He not with Him also freely give us all things?

Remember God's Word about us in Jeremiah 29:11, **For I know the thoughts that I think toward you, says the LORD, thoughts of peace and not of evil, to give you a future and a hope?** The Hebrew word for "know" is an incredible word. It gives us a picture of knowing someone on the most intimate level possible.[2] The Hebrew word for "thoughts" is another interesting word. It can be understood as "contrivances, machines, or inventions."[3] We can see that God knows us to the very core of our being, and He sees every detail of the plan and purpose of our lives. He even sees the physical means by which He will get us where He wants us to go.

The Hebrew word for "peace," *shalom,* sets the tone for all of God's plans and purposes. He desires not only to accomplish something great in us and through us, but He wants to do it in a very specific manner: by peace! *Shalom* conveys safety, well-being, happiness, health, and prosperity.[4] Then finally, the Hebrew word for "hope" literally means a "cord," but figuratively means "an expectation."[5] The *King James Version* translates it, "an expected end."[6]

---

[2] *Strong's Exhaustive Concordance of the Bible,* "Hebrew and Chaldee Dictionary," by J. B. Strong (Atlanta: Thomas Nelson Publishers, 1990) #3045, p. 47.

[3] Ibid., #4284, p. 65.

[4] Ibid., #7965, p. 116.

[5] Ibid., #8615, p. 126.

[6] Ibid., #319, p. 11.

In effect, God is saying, "I know you better than anyone in the universe knows you, and I have seen the operation and the outcome of the plan I have put into action for you. If you take hold of the cord of hope with hands of faith, you can draw your blessings unto yourself. What you desire, hope for, and long for is on the way!"

Seeing the Impossible

Imagine you are a three-year-old being led by your dad through the crowded midway of the state fair. All you can see is a maze of legs, and you're getting tired. You want to go home, sit down, or stop at a brightly lit attraction. But your father stands tall above the crowd and can see the merry-go-round up ahead. He's leading you right to a wonderful, exciting experience, but you can't see it yet. "Trust me," he says.

Our heavenly Father has our dream destination in sight, but to get there we must accept His definition of who we are and obey His every direction. Too many people see themselves through the eyes of other people. They assume the role people assign to them and accept the value others place on them. They end up doing what others think they should do instead of what God wants them to do. Too many people internalize an inferiority complex that causes them to yield ground when challenged by those they wish to please or impress.

What's worse, some people have appointed themselves to be dream killers. They're good at seeking out our most precious dreams and doing their best to destroy them. They know that God-given dreams are fragile when new, and they've perfected their technique of taking just the right comment, with just the right roll of the eyes, to kill our dreams before we can reach them.

In Numbers 13:33, the children of Israel had sent scouts to check out the Promised Land. Most of the spies reported to Moses, "We saw great, huge giants and felt like grasshoppers." God had just shown His power to deliver them, both in Egypt and at the Red Sea. He had promised them the Promised Land, but rather than allowing God to define them, they allowed their enemies and ten unbelieving, faithless spies to tell them who they were.

We must never forget that whenever God assigns a role, He enables us to play it. In Judges the Angel of the Lord recruited Gideon, who was hiding from his enemies, by saying:

> "The LORD is with you, you mighty man of valor!"
>
> . . . Then the LORD turned to him and said, "Go in this might of yours, and you shall save Israel from the hand of the Midianites. Have I not sent you?"
>
> So he said to Him, "O my Lord, how can I save Israel? Indeed my clan is the weakest in Manasseh, and I am the least in my father's house."
>
> And the LORD said to him, "Surely I will be with you, and you shall defeat the Midianites as one man."
>
> Judges 6:12,14-16

Sure enough, when God was through, Gideon had shown himself to be a mighty man of valor, and his enemies — who also happened to be God's enemies — had been defeated. This points out another aspect of God-given dreams. God always makes the dream bigger than we are. He always places us before something that we can't handle by ourselves. He always gives us a challenge that is impossible by human standards. He always waits until its too late and we don't have enough. He stands us before Goliaths, fiery furnaces, lions' dens, and unbeatable odds so that we will rely on Him. In this way, no one can take His glory. He always provides for the miracle margin, but God brings us face-to-face with the impossible so He can get the glory.

God will even replace possible dreams with dreams that seem impossible. John Croyle was a hot-shot defensive end at the University of Alabama during Bear Bryant's glory years. Not surprisingly, making it big in the NFL was John's dream from his childhood. Throughout his college career, professional football scouts were eyeing him closely. His dreams of a pro career were well on their way toward coming true.

The summer after his sophomore year, however, things began to change. John worked as a counselor in a Christian summer camp for boys, where he discovered his real talent. He had an amazing gift for making kids who felt worthless feel worthy and loved. It's a rare gift, and he felt called to share it. But how?

After years of football dreams, Croyle began to see a far bigger dream, a dream of helping these unwanted, abused, and abandoned kids to have a home of their own, where they'd be loved and cared for without regard to background, color, or past troubles. Despite the fact that he had no money and no place to house any kids, he focused on his new, impossible dream. He told everyone he knew about his plans.

The dream of a boys' home seemed so impossible, Croyle's friends told him he should just defer it and go play a few years in the NFL to earn enough money to fund his ranch. But Croyle refused the draft. He wouldn't be sidetracked from his new God-given dream. He stuck with it. He scraped together just enough money for a down payment on a dilapidated farm in Alabama and started the Big Oak Ranch with five boys. Over the next twenty years, John Croyle loved, disciplined, hugged, and helped more than twelve hundred kids—because he kept dreaming his God-given, impossible dream and refused to go back to his own possible dream.

Giving God Glory

When the dream is hard but possible, the dreamer gets the glory.

When the dream is absolutely impossible, God gets the glory.

God does not give us dreams to accomplish just so we can get a big head over our success. He does it so people will know there is a God and that He is a rewarder of those who diligently seek Him. Our success in accomplishing something impossible brings Him glory, and the more crazy and unlikely the dream, the better!

> *The foolishness of God is wiser than men, and the weakness of God is stronger than men.*

> *For you see your calling, brethren, that not many wise according to the flesh, not many mighty, not many noble, are called.*

> *But God has chosen the foolish things of the world to put*
> *to shame the wise, and God has chosen the weak things of the*
> *world to put to shame the things which are mighty;*
>
> *and the base things of the world and the things which are*
> *despised God has chosen, and the things which are not, to*
> *bring to nothing the things that are,*
>
> *that no flesh should glory in His presence.*

1 Corinthians 1:25-29

This is why it is so important to praise God, give Him thanks, and point any glory toward Him. When people are not appreciated, they sometimes back off so that they will be missed and their presence will be more appreciated. When we don't pray and praise God, He allows us to get into a predicament so that we'll have to pray; and when He brings us out, we have to praise Him! Sometimes, He lets things happen so He can get our attention, get us in line, and make us play our role. If we had praised and had given Him glory, we might have avoided some difficult times.

> *I am the LORD, that is My name;*
> *And My glory I will not give to another,*
> *Nor My praise to carved images.*

Isaiah 42:8

God also tests us to see if we have learned our lesson well. You see, **Without faith it is impossible to please Him** (Hebrews 11:6). And faith is most apparent amid the storms and trials of life. We know the faith of great men and women of God, either because of their faithfulness and confidence amid their trials or because of their willingness to go beyond others in their service of God. If they had not had a storm, if they had not gone beyond, we would never have known of their faith. The only reason we talk about Job is the fact that he trusted God after he lost everything. He confidently said,

> But He knows the way that I take;
> When He has tested me, I shall come forth as gold.

Job 23:10

The only reason we know of the widow of Zarephath (see 1 Kings 17) is that she was willing to give her last morsel of food to the prophet during a famine. She went beyond where others were willing to go. Because of her faith, God gave her more than enough. When God blesses us as we reach for our dream, He expects us to go beyond others in giving and service. Jesus says in Luke 12:48:

> "For everyone to whom much is given, from him much will be required; and to whom much has been committed, of him they will ask the more."

The apostle Paul learned the art of going through storms and going beyond. He said in Philippians 4:11-13:

> Not that I speak in regard to need, for I have learned in whatever state I am, to be content:

> I know how to be abased, and I know how to abound. Everywhere and in all things I have learned both to be full and to be hungry, both to abound and to suffer need.

I can do all things through Christ who strengthens me.

The Lord says in Isaiah 14:24,

"Surely, as I have thought, so it shall come to pass,
And as I have purposed, so it shall stand."

As we struggle along with our eyes on the dream, remember that we have a Comforter who comes alongside us to remind us that we are in the Father's hands:

The Spirit Himself bears witness with our spirit that we
are children of God,

and if children, then heirs — heirs of God and joint heirs
with Christ, if indeed we suffer with Him, that we may also be
glorified together.

Romans 8:16-17

Although we can't always see the wonderful things God has in store for us, we continue to trust Him and follow His dream. We dare not limit our belief in God's dreams for us by our own shortsighted definition of our abilities because He **is able to do exceedingly abundantly above all that we ask or think, according to the power that works in us** (Ephesians 3:20).

Oh, little lame duck, let me tell you about a man who begged for alms beside the gate called Beautiful. Like you, little duck, he had been lame from birth. As he was begging, Peter and John passed by. Knowing God's power to redefine the roles of those who believe, Peter said,

*"Silver and gold I do not have, but what I do have I give
you: In the name of Jesus Christ of Nazareth, rise up and walk."*

Acts 3:6

And you know, little duck, he walked!

We must not allow anyone but God to assign our roles to us,
especially not the devil. Would we let our track coach assign us
the job of javelin *catcher?* No, that's a dead-end job, and so are all
the roles the devil would assign us. He hates us and wants to
destroy us. If we play along with him, he will succeed. We must
also stop letting *people* limit our dreams for us and assign our
roles to us. Like the devil, most of the time they just want to use
us for their own devices, make us what they want us to be, and
have us join them in their misery.

Only our Father in heaven can show us who we are and bring
complete fulfillment and joy to our lives. We must hold fast to the
dreams He places in our hearts and persevere against the flow of
the world, moving according to God's Spirit and His Word.

God Shows *the* Way

Chapter 5

Unless Your law had been my delight,
I would then have perished in my affliction.

I will never forget Your precepts,
For by them You have given me life.

Psalm 119:92-93

The author of this psalm was David, the man who had a heart after God, but David also loved and reverenced God's Word. When he was a young man, tending the sheep of his father, the prophet Samuel came to David and gave him a dream. Samuel anointed him to be king of Israel in place of Saul, who had disobeyed God and proved himself unfit to rule by his unwillingness to repent. Being king was a big dream for David, and a big dream like this required him to have wisdom and courage far beyond his years. In some situations, the wrong decisions could have killed him or made him unfit for kingship.

When Saul became aware that God's anointing had left him and now rested upon David, he became insanely jealous and pursued David relentlessly, trying to kill him. David was forced to live in the wilderness, living from cave to cave, fleeing for his life. Then one day, who should walk into the cave where David was hiding but Saul. At that critical moment, David was faced with a choice. His men urged him to kill Saul while he was in a vulnerable position. David had the perfect opportunity to rid himself of the man who wanted to destroy him. But David also knew the Law of the Lord, and he said to his followers:

> *"The LORD forbid that I should do this thing to my master,
> the LORD's anointed, to stretch out my hand against him,
> seeing he is the anointed of the LORD."*

1 Samuel 24:6

David's faithfulness to God's Law was the reason God chose him to be king instead of Saul, who had shown no regard for His commands. David refused to kill Saul because he knew only the Lord had that right. He wouldn't have passed this crucial test on the way to his God-given dream if he had not understood the way God operated in making dreams come true.

If we were taking a long journey into uncharted waters, wouldn't we place a high value on a set of clear directions from someone who had led many others to their destination? Well, we have such a guidebook, and God has given us the same directions He gave David. As we explore the way to reach our God-given dreams, He has given us the same map to follow.

The Law of the Lord

The 119th Psalm speaks of the privileges and happiness of those who observe the Law of the Lord. That Law is called by various names to show its diverse excellencies: testimonies, commandments, precepts, word, law, ways, truth, judgments, righteousness, and statutes. When we sum up these concepts or titles under the heading, "the Law of God," it seems to make them restrictive, controlling, and oppressive. Yet nothing could be further from the mind or the intent of God. God intends for His Law to be liberating, enlightening, and life-enhancing. He intends for His Law to help us find our way to the dreams He gives us.

When we know the laws of our nation, we know our rights, our protections under the law, our privileges, our sources of relief, our restrictions, and our prohibitions. When we don't know the law, we are likely not only to transgress it, but we're also likely to miss out on many of the privileges that are legally ours. So it is with the Law of God. The Law of God tells us not only what we must not do, it tells us about our Lord and King. It tells us who we are, what wonderful privileges are ours, and what is the best and wisest course through time and eternity.

The Law of God might also be called the Word of God or the wisdom of God. When we use the word "wisdom," we are inclined to conceive of the matter altogether differently than when we use the word "law." Most people perceive the Law of God as "Thou shalt not . . . , thou shalt not. . . ." But when we say the *wisdom* of God, we think of a vital tool that allows us to achieve success and fulfillment in life.

Wisdom is said to be the ability to judge correctly and to follow the best course of action. It is based on knowledge and understanding of that knowledge, which then dictates the best attitude and plan of action. *Knowledge* is to be acquainted with the facts and realities, *understanding* is the ability to see the relationship between the realities, and *wisdom* is the ability to know the best thing to do or to think and then to do it.

In a way, the laws of our nation might be called the wisdom of our nation. Our constitution is probably the best of any nation in the world. But if the laws of our nation are the wisdom of our nation, then we must conclude that we are not very wise. I say this because amendments have had to be passed, new laws are constantly being legislated, and a host of men and women are paid large sums of money to issue a myriad of new edicts, ordinances, and statues.

If our laws were so wise, they would not have to be changed so much. Many of them were unjust because they excluded and failed to mention so many of God's children: God's Native American children, God's black children, and God's female children. Even now, the focus of our national laws changes every time a different political party obtains a voting majority. Man-made laws have to change all the time, so we are not all that wise. But let's deal with the question, "Is God wise enough to direct our paths?" To that question we must answer, "Yes, God is all wise. God is infinitely wise. His laws never have to change."

Great is our Lord, and mighty in power;
His understanding is infinite.

Psalm 147:5

God's Wisdom

The LORD by wisdom founded the earth;
By understanding He established the heavens;

By His knowledge the depths were broken up,
And clouds drop down the dew.

Proverbs 3:19-20

Every inhabitant on this earth, from humans to worms, is a testimony to the wisdom of God. We are fearfully and wonderfully made. The more scientists delve into the inner workings of life on earth, the more they marvel at the incredible wisdom of its design. Even secular scientists who believe we evolved from protozoa can't explain the brilliant design of the DNA sequences that make up all life. But the Word of God reveals the truth: **In the beginning God . . .** (Genesis 1:1). In Psalm 19, the Bible confirms this by saying, in verse 1, **The heavens declare the glory of God;/And the firmament shows His handiwork.** But further on in Psalm 19 David goes on to imply that the Word of God is a product of that same wisdom by which the worlds were made:

The law of the LORD is perfect, converting the soul;
The testimony of the LORD is sure, making wise the simple;

The statutes of the LORD are right, rejoicing the heart;
The commandment of the LORD is pure, enlightening the eyes;

The fear of the LORD is clean, enduring forever;
The judgments of the LORD are true and righteous altogether.

Psalm 19:7-9

I believe that puts to rest the recurring lie that the Bible was concocted by a series of ghostwriters. I could write a whole book on the divine origin of God's Word and how it has stood the

God intends for His Law to
be liberating, enlightening,
and life-enhancing.
He intends for His Law
to help us find our way
to the dreams He gives us.

tests of time and criticism, but at this point it is sufficient to say that God's Word is exactly what God says it is: It is the Word of God written through Spirit-led men:

> *knowing this first, that no prophecy of Scripture is of any private interpretation,*
>
> *for prophecy never came by the will of man, but holy men of God spoke as they were moved by the Holy Spirit.*
>
> 2 Peter 1:20-21

We cannot simply pick and choose which parts of the Bible we want to accept. A group of alleged Bible scholars recently sat down to determine just how much of the Bible they, in their estimation, could believe was really true. These individuals, educated far beyond wisdom, determined that most of the Bible was unreliable and denied Jesus' virgin birth, His miracles, and His resurrection. What unmitigated arrogance! How can we, in our feeble wisdom, dare to negate parts of God's Word simply because we can't wrap our little finite brains around those aspects of an infinite God? Take it all or take a hike, critics—you simply aren't that smart!

We need to humble ourselves and understand that God is so much wiser than we are. Any criticism we could have of God or His Word merely reveals our foolishness and utter lack of wisdom because the foolishness of God is wiser than men, and the weakness of God is stronger than men. (See 1 Corinthians 1:25.) However, men tend to get cocky when they do wonderful things like fly to the moon, split the atom, and discover the secrets of the human genome. We often fail to recognize that, as much as we have seen and done, God's wisdom is as high above ours as are the heavens above the earth. After all, who designed and spoke into existence the human genome that we tried so hard to figure out?

In our presumed wisdom, then, we've tended to go our own way, thinking we are wise enough to run our own lives. We are like a toddler who sits in his car seat and watches his mom drive the family car. After two years of observing, he feels confident that he's smart enough to drive. Is he? Of course not. Well then, are we smart enough to grab the steering wheel of our own lives to aim for and reach a destination that only God knows?

> *There is a way that seems right to a man,*
> *But its end is the way of death.*

> Proverbs 14:12

How many times do we need to wind up spinning off the road into another ditch to figure out that every time we grab control of our lives from God, we crash? Is this wisdom? Is this the way to reach our dreams? The only way to reach our destination, our dream, is to leave God and His Word in control of our lives.

> *Trust in the LORD with all your heart,*
> *And lean not on your own understanding;*

> *In all your ways acknowledge Him,*
> *And He shall direct your paths.*

> *Do not be wise in your own eyes;*
> *Fear the LORD and depart from evil.*

How can we, in our
feeble wisdom, dare to negate
parts of God's Word simply
because we can't wrap our little
finite brains around those
aspects of an infinite God?

It will be health to your flesh,
And strength to your bones.

Proverbs 3:5-8

Some people think that we're weak because we depend on the wisdom of God for guidance. They clearly don't know how powerful the wisdom contained in God's Word is! They attempt to place sources of human wisdom on the same level as the Bible. They'd like to think that psychology, the Koran, psychics, and extra-biblical "gospels" have the same value in directing our lives as does the Word of God. When we choose to follow the wisdom of God and fly in the face of human wisdom, we show the power of God's Word to the world. When we declare the Word over a subject, we carve through all the hogwash, says the writer of Hebrews:

For the word of God is living and powerful, and sharper
than any two-edged sword, piercing even to the division of soul
and spirit, and of joints and marrow, and is a discerner of the
thoughts and intents of the heart.

Hebrews 4:12

Speaking the Word of God always makes some people think—and it always makes some people mad! We ought to be used to both reactions by now. Moreover, we ought to know it is the only solid rock on which to stand. More than any man-made wisdom, God's Word is dependable. The fifteenth-century French mystic, Nostradamus, was in the news because he predicted that a terrible cataclysm would occur in July 1999. Well, July 1999 passed and nothing much happened. It was just one more total strikeout for an alleged prophet whose credibility should have been dismissed long ago.

On the other hand, biblical prophecy and wisdom are inerrant. While we may not know the exact details, we can depend on the Word of God to be a rock of reliability.

> *having been born again, not of corruptible seed but incorruptible, through the word of God which lives and abides forever,*
>
> *because "All flesh is as grass,*
> *And all the glory of man as the flower of the grass.*
> *The grass withers,*
> *And its flower falls away,*
>
> *"But the word of the LORD endures forever."*
> *Now this is the word which by the gospel*
> *was preached to you.*

1 Peter 1:23-25

God's Light

> *Your word is a lamp to my feet*
> *And a light to my path.*

Psalm 119:105

Not only is the Word of God utterly reliable, people desire and seek after God's wisdom because in it He shows the faithful the way to great reward. The Word lights our path in this dark, confusing world and keeps us free of sin and evil.

More to be desired are they than gold,
Yea, than much fine gold;
Sweeter also than honey and the honeycomb.

Moreover by them Your servant is warned,
And in keeping them there is great reward.

Who can understand his errors?
Cleanse me from secret faults.

Keep back Your servant also from presumptuous sins;
Let them not have dominion over me.
Then I shall be blameless,
And I shall be innocent of great transgression.

Let the words of my mouth and the meditation of my heart
Be acceptable in Your sight,
O LORD, my strength and my Redeemer.

Psalm 19:10-14

The way for us to avail ourselves of God's superior wisdom and the reward it contains is revealed to us in His Word. It's there for us to consult at any time, on any subject, for any purpose. When we're wrong, it makes us right. When we're weak, it makes us strong. When we're lost, it shows us the way.

from childhood you have known the Holy Scriptures,
which are able to make you wise for salvation through faith
which is in Christ Jesus.

All Scripture is given by inspiration of God, and is
profitable for doctrine, for reproof, for correction, for instruc-
tion in righteousness,

*that the man of God may be complete, thoroughly equipped
for every good work.*

2 Timothy 3:15-17

"But we've read a lot of the Bible, and hear it preached every
Sunday. Why do we still mess up?" Too many Christians merely
have a surface knowledge of the Bible. They know the Sunday-
school stories, they've memorized a few promises, but they don't
have that deep knowledge of the Word that can only come by
daily study, meditation, and prayer.

*Study to shew thyself approved unto God, a workman that
needeth not to be ashamed, rightly dividing the word of truth.*

2 Timothy 2:15 KJV

Even those who have made the effort to read a chapter in the
Bible each day may not benefit as they should because they're
doing it as a religious exercise, another chore to be checked off
on their to-do list. They read hurriedly, without prayer, reflection, or meditation, then zip off to the next item on their day's
agenda. But the folk who follow hard after God to attain their
God-given dreams read the Word hungrily, searching for the face
of God in His Word. They do an exhaustive study on a concept
like holiness, then prayerfully compare their lives to what
they've read and reflect on the discrepancies. They make changes
in their lives according to the discrepancies the Word shows.
They repent in sorrow and in reverential fear of a holy and righteous God. Then they pick up the Word again to stay pure in that
area and begin to purify another area of their lives.

When we go wrong, it's most likely because we didn't know what God said in His Word about the subject, or we didn't believe He meant what He said. But just as it is in civil court, ignorance of the law is no defense. When the Sadducees were trying to trick Jesus with the Word, they showed that they only had a surface knowledge of the Law. Jesus answered and said to them,

> *"You are mistaken, not knowing the Scriptures nor the power of God."*

Matthew 22:29

When we truly abide in God's Word, as Jesus exhorted us in John 8:31-32, then we will know the truth and the truth will make us free. When we walk in the light with Jesus, all the wisdom of God is available to us. His light fills us with peace and joy at the expectation of our dreams coming true, and we can see where we're going and how to get there!

The Jesus Factor

This will be a hard word to some folk, but a superficial, surface knowledge of the Word of God leads Christians to become comfortable in their sin. Far too many believers use what they think is the covering of God's grace and love as simply an excuse for their own disobedience. They feel they're free to disobey God whenever obedience is uncomfortable or inconvenient, comforting themselves with the notion that the grace of God will cover their disobedience. The words "sin" and "repentance" never come up.

When this attitude, commonly termed "greasy grace," shows up in a church, we see Christians pursue worldly dreams and pleasures rather than God-given dreams. They become lustful, hard-hearted, self-willed, and greedy. They grab the things of the world and call them the blessings of the Lord. Sadly, they often don't get corrected from the pulpit because any "prosperity" they achieve is interpreted as God's blessing on their lives — especially if they tithe!

It seems that many in the Church have exchanged *belief* for *agreement*. They agree to accept Jesus as Savior, but do not believe on Him as their Lord and Master. Some folk are moved emotionally to pray the sinner's prayer, but they never turn away from their disobedience. They give mental assent to the existence of Jesus without having a real change of heart. They intellectually agree that Jesus is their Savior, but they never allow Him to become Lord of their lives. If Jesus is only our Savior and not the Lord of our lives, we cannot expect to attain our God-given dreams. We'll follow our lusts every time. We must take God's Law, His Word, and do what it says. James admonishes us:

> *But be doers of the word, and not hearers only, deceiving yourselves.*
>
> *For if anyone is a hearer of the word and not a doer, he is like a man observing his natural face in a mirror;*
>
> *for he observes himself, goes away, and immediately forgets what kind of man he was.*

> *But he who looks into the perfect law of liberty and contin-*
> *ues in it, and is not a forgetful hearer but a doer of the work,*
> *this one will be blessed in what he does.*

> James 1:22-25

God's wisdom is revealed to us not only in His Word, but in His Son, Jesus Christ. Today's worldwide ecumenical movement seems to want to minimize talk of Jesus as being divisive. Talking about God is safe, but talking about Jesus stirs up trouble. The truth is, we cannot talk about God's wisdom without lifting up Jesus, who is **made unto us wisdom** (1 Corinthians 1:30 KJV). By maintaining a close relationship with Jesus, we avail ourselves of God's great wisdom.

> *God, who at various times and in various ways spoke in*
> *time past to the fathers by the prophets,*

> *has in these last days spoken to us by His Son, whom He*
> *has appointed heir of all things, through whom also He made*
> *the worlds;*

> *who being the brightness of His glory and the express*
> *image of His person, and upholding all things by the word of*
> *His power, when He had by Himself purged our sins, sat down*
> *at the right hand of the Majesty on high.*

> Hebrews 1:1-3

Just as following God-given dreams is foolishness to the world, the fact that we worship a God who allowed His Son to be killed sounds crazy to the unsaved world. They don't understand the atoning sacrifice of Jesus or the people who follow Him, so we're not surprised when they don't share our enthusiasm for God's Word, His way of doing things, or His wonderful plan for our lives.

> *For since, in the wisdom of God, the world through wisdom did not know God, it pleased God through the foolishness of the message preached to save those who believe.*
>
> *For Jews request a sign, and Greeks seek after wisdom;*
>
> *but we preach Christ crucified, to the Jews a stumbling block and to the Greeks foolishness,*
>
> *but to those who are called, both Jews and Greeks, Christ the power of God and the wisdom of God.*
>
> 1 Corinthians 1:21-24

Did you realize that Jesus is also God's spoken Word to us? To understand the wonderful interaction among Jesus, God, and the Word, prayerfully read and reflect on these first few verses of the book of John:

> *In the beginning was the Word, and the Word was with God, and the Word was God.*
>
> *He was in the beginning with God.*
>
> *All things were made through Him, and without Him nothing was made that was made.*
>
> *In Him was life, and the life was the light of men. . . .*
>
> *He was in the world, and the world was made through Him, and the world did not know Him.*
>
> *He came to His own, and His own did not receive Him.*

But as many as received Him, to them He gave the right to become children of God, to those who believe in His name. . . .

And the Word became flesh and dwelt among us, and we beheld His glory, the glory as of the only begotten of the Father, full of grace and truth.

John 1:1-4,10-12,14

Until we make God's Law, God's Word, and God's Son our delight, we will never be able to fully comprehend, much less attain, God's greatest dreams for our lives. To be sure, it will require work on our part, just as Joseph had to work in Potiphar's house. And just as Joseph resisted Potiphar's wife, reaching our dreams will require hard-headed faithfulness to resist the errant advice of godless people and our own lustful desires.

Reaching our God-given dreams is impossible to do alone, but we are not alone! Not only is God with us, but He gives us His Word and His wisdom to show us the way. Yes, when we first encounter a God-given, impossible dream, we sigh and say, "The journey is too far, too mysterious, with too many unknowns." But then we hear the still, small voice inside us whisper firmly, "God's Law, His Word, and His wisdom will lead you. All you must do is follow!"

How Tough *Are* You?

Chapter 6

Have you ever seen new recruits for the U. S. Navy SEALs in their basic training? Striving to be naval commandos, they go through weeks of the most incredibly demanding regimen that includes hours spent swimming in cold water, thousands of push-ups and sit-ups, and miles and miles of running in sand. Pushed to the limits of their physical and mental endurance and beyond, seven out of ten men quit before they finish. Those who survive are trained to be America's greatest secret warriors. The SEAL instructors nearly kill these young men in training because they know the strength of a person is not revealed by how they function when demands are low and conditions are ideal. Courage and character are revealed under stress.

Pressure Builds Character

A person's ability to survive and attain their God-given dreams is not determined by how that person deals with normal everyday living. Even the term *"survive"* implies that one has confronted something that might well have taken them out, but they outlasted it and kept on living. Strength and ability are manifested and developed when the burden is heavy and the conditions are complicated and adverse. You can't succeed in becoming a great athlete or a seasoned sea captain by sitting in an easy chair in front of the television. Come to think of it, there's not much you can become sitting in an easy chair in front of a television—except fat!

A great athlete is revealed only after the most difficult of opponents and contests have been endured and conquered. A great sea captain is revealed only after he has successfully stood at his command through many violent storms and attacks. Likewise, to accomplish our God-given dreams, we would do well to prepare for the unexpected, the difficult, and the insurmountable. If we expect to last and survive, we must be ready to deal with periods of diminishing returns, drought, scarcity, trouble, distress, and affliction.

Even without God-given, impossible dreams, life is filled with uncertainty. This is why people have life insurance, automobile insurance, homeowner's insurance, and health insurance. We know that during our lifetime there is the possibility that we may get sick, we may be injured, we may have an automobile accident, the house may catch fire, and sooner or later we're guaranteed to die. Adversity is a given in the equation of life on planet earth.

Pressure is a sure thing for all human beings. On the way to our destination of God-given dreams, we're going to pass through situations and circumstances which will bring pressure to bear on our faith and trust in God. Pressure comes in the forms of poverty, difficult and even evil people, tormenting spirits, sickness, and persecution. Pressure means persistent pain or distress. Although we all want to reach our dreams, no one enjoys the pressures which accompany them. But pressure is inevitable, and during times of pressure we can be strengthened in the Lord and grow up in God.

When you squeeze something, you find out what is in it. When life squeezes us, the devil attempts to torment us, and our flesh begins to scream from the discomfort, we find out what's in us. Does whining, complaining, doubt, and unbelief come out when we are squeezed by the trials of life? Or do we reach deeper into the Spirit of Truth, grab hold of the revelation of God's Word for that moment of pressure, and boldly proclaim and firmly stand on what God has to say about our situation?

When pressure comes, our whole being should thrill at the knowledge that we have another opportunity for God to work in us and through us. When pressure comes, we should rejoice at the certainty that He will take us to the next level to achieve the next step in realizing the dreams He has placed in our hearts. Pressure makes us tough in God.

Wilderness Training

There are many Christians today, especially in America, whose survival is still jeopardized when everything is all right. They can hardly deal with mundane, day-to-day living. Are you one of those persons who has food to eat, clothes to wear, a place to sleep, a church, and good health, but still life is unbearable for you? What are you going to do if it really gets rough and tough? How will you react when real pressure falls upon you? Proverbs 24:10 says: **If you faint in the day of adversity, your strength is small.** If we faint in the face of no adversity, or little adversity, our strength must be almost nonexistent! We hear the same warning in Jeremiah 12:5:

> *"If you have run with the footmen, and they have*
> *wearied you,*
> *Then how can you contend with horses?*
> *And if in the land of peace,*
> *In which you trusted, they wearied you,*
> *Then how will you do in the floodplain of the Jordan?"*

Weak, unstable people don't just hurt the Church and the work of the Lord. When we tolerate spiritual mediocrity within ourselves, we guarantee that we will be devastated when the real tests come—and they will come! If we have little time for church, if we don't practice consistent godly living and godly giving, where will we be when the time comes for the real spiritual champions to step forth for service?

When there is a lack of commitment, strength, and all-out zeal for God in believers, even the smallest of projects that most churches launch is like pulling teeth and amputating limbs. Because they are selfish and self-centered, they would rather die than give a thousand dollars to the church, yet they wear a thousand dollars' worth of clothes, shoes, hats, and jewelry every time they walk through the church doors. And let's not even think about how many hours believers spend on sports, hobbies, movies, and other entertainments—but they have no time to study the Bible, pray, have family devotions, or volunteer in the Sunday school.

The children of Israel were weak in faith and self-centered instead of God-centered. As a result God had to keep them in the wilderness for forty years instead of taking them into the

Promised Land. When they left Egypt, they were rich. God had caused the Egyptians to give them great treasures. Then He showed His power and delivered them by pushing back the Red Sea and destroying their enemies. But they still had that slave mentality, that defeatist attitude. So when they came to the land of Canaan, which was flowing with milk and honey, they were afraid of the giants in the land. They were afraid even when they knew they had the one and only God on their side. They were too weak to enter into the land of their dreams.

God kept Israel in the wilderness until they were ready to be good soldiers. This is where He sought to make them tough in Him. They had to work on their faith to become an army that could overcome the enemy by trusting Him, no matter how difficult or adverse the circumstances. As the Marines say, "It's better to sweat in training than bleed in battle!" God might well have said, "It's going to be tough in the Promised Land. It will take guts and faith to take what I have given to you, so I can't let you go in until you are ready."

> "And you shall remember that the LORD your God led you all the way these forty years in the wilderness, to humble you and test you, to know what was in your heart, whether you would keep His commandments or not.
>
> "So He humbled you, allowed you to hunger, and fed you with manna which you did not know nor did your fathers know, that He might make you know that man shall not live by bread alone; but man lives by every word that proceeds from the mouth of the LORD."
>
> Deuteronomy 8:2-3

Courage and
character are revealed
under stress.

God had a good end in store for Israel, but He had to get them ready, and some would never be ready. One of the main reasons they were fearful and unbelieving was that they were more concerned about their own personal welfare and private success than they were about God's eternal purposes and plans. When He judged their doubt and unbelief, they did not fall on their faces and repent. The Bible tells us they knew they had sinned, but they tried to "prove" themselves by taking the action they should have taken in faith the day before. Rather than a true, godly sorrow at their lack of trust in God, they felt the sting of a missed opportunity and decided to go into the Promised Land immediately. Moses warned them that they would not succeed, that God's decree to wander in the wilderness was now their destiny, but they persisted in their folly. This is what occurred:

> *And they rose early in the morning and went up to the top of the mountain, saying, "Here we are, and we will go up to the place which the LORD has promised, for we have sinned!"*
>
> *And Moses said, "Now why do you transgress the command of the LORD? For this will not succeed.*
>
> *"Do not go up, lest you be defeated by your enemies, for the LORD is not among you.*
>
> *"For the Amalekites and the Canaanites are there before you, and you shall fall by the sword; because you have turned away from the LORD, the LORD will not be with you."*
>
> *But they presumed to go up to the mountaintop. Nevertheless, neither the ark of the covenant of the LORD nor Moses departed from the camp.*

Then the Amalekites and the Canaanites who dwelt in that mountain came down and attacked them, and drove them back as far as Hormah.

Numbers 14:40-45

The enemy drove Israel back because when they decided to act, it came from a selfish motive. God could do nothing but stand by and watch their defeat. The lessons for us are obvious. First, when we see we have sinned, disobeyed, or not trusted God in some way, we must repent. We must seek His face, get into the secret place of the Most High, and find His wisdom and grace for our time of need. Second, as we seek our God-given dreams, we must not rush into places and situations, grabbing onto new positions and responsibilities, until we're ready for the battles that will come. We must have God's plan and carry it out in His timing to be successful.

First Things First

Do you seem to be in the wilderness on the way to your dream? Do you feel that you're going round and round, getting nowhere fast? I urge you to go to God and ask Him, "Why are You keeping me at this level so long? What is it that prevents me from going to the next level?" It may well be that you can't go to the next level because God sees that you simply aren't ready for the next level. You haven't learned the lesson He intended you to learn from the current pressure. If you want to go to college, you must pass high school first!

We cannot realize our dreams without making sure we have the right set of priorities. When we major in the minors, we can lose our bearings and wander in circles. What should be first in our Christian walk? That's an easy one:

> *"But seek first the kingdom of God and His righteousness, and all these things shall be added to you."*
>
> Matthew 6:33

Our first priority must be the will, the rule, and the righteousness of God in our lives. Does anything in life come before the kingdom? Do family matters come before the things of God? Does church work come before prayer and Bible study? When God knows our relationship with Him takes first priority in our lives, He will advance us, promote us, and entrust us with His resources. We show our love for God by putting *His* priorities first. Then He says, "If you love Me and pursue My purposes, then I will see to it that all things you encounter work for your good."

> *And we know that all things work together for good to those who love God, to those who are the called according to His purpose.*
>
> Romans 8:28

We are not really ready to be blessed until blessings are not our first priority. Seeking God must be first, then blessings and achievement will follow. We can truly say that we are ready to be blessed when we can say in all honesty, "The greatest thing in all my life is loving God, serving God, and knowing God." The

We are not really
ready to be blessed
until blessings are not
our first priority.

apostle Paul was someone who realized his God-given dreams. He shared this truth with the Philippians:

> *But what things were gain to me, these I have counted loss for Christ.*
>
> *Yet indeed I also count all things loss for the excellence of the knowledge of Christ Jesus my Lord, for whom I have suffered the loss of all things, and count them as rubbish, that I may gain Christ*
>
> *and be found in Him, not having my own righteousness, which is from the law, but that which is through faith in Christ, the righteousness which is from God by faith;*
>
> *that I may know Him and the power of His resurrection, and the fellowship of His sufferings.*
>
> Philippians 3:7-10

If you say, "I'm already blessed," I would say that you may *think* you're blessed, but you're not blessed like you could be! We cannot comprehend the marvelous plans God has for us. Joseph dreamed that his brothers would bow to him, but he never dreamed he would be second only to Pharaoh in the land of Egypt, or that he would not only save his whole family from starvation but vastly increase their wealth.

> *"Eye has not seen, nor ear heard,*
> *Nor have entered into the heart of man*
> *The things which God has prepared for those who love Him."*
>
> 1 Corinthians 2:9

We think on a human scale, but God plans on a much vaster scale, His divine, eternal scale. Our dreams are too little! However, by putting God first in all areas of our lives, we will begin to see the bigger picture and the greater dream.

New Level, New Devil

As we put God first and begin to climb to new levels of success in realizing our dreams, we face new and different challenges. A wise soul once observed, "New level, new devil." I have found that the devil uses a different strategy against us at each new level we attain. We must battle against and defeat a stronger and more cunning demon at each level of our faith walk. If the devil of this present level is walking all over us, what do we think that next devil, on the next level, is going to do to us? We had better beat the devil on this level because when we get to the next level there will be a new devil, and then we will be dealing with two of them! A victory on this present level will help us get the victory on the next level. As a matter of fact, if we just deal with the present, God will take care of tomorrow.

With new blessings come new challenges, problems, and persecutions. We don't like to talk about persecutions, but I know that the strongest Christians in the world are the ones under the most persecution, so I'm not going to run when it comes. I'm expecting it because Jesus told me to expect it:

> *So Jesus answered and said, "Assuredly, I say to you, there is no one who has left house or brothers or sisters or father or mother or wife or children or lands, for My sake and the gospel's,*

"who shall not receive a hundredfold now in this time —
houses and brothers and sisters and mothers and children and
lands, with persecutions *— and in the age to come, eternal life."*

Mark 10:29-30 (emphasis mine)

Does it frighten you to think of persecutions and afflictions coming with the achievement of your dreams? Sometimes, if we knew what the new level was going to bring with it, we would almost say, "No thank You, Lord! If You don't mind, I'd like to stay right where I am." However, we can't stand still and be any good to the kingdom of God. Water that stays where it is soon gets stagnant, begins to stink, and eventually becomes no good to anyone. Do we want to be a flowing river or a smelly mud puddle?

We'll never reach our God-given dreams if we stay in our nice, cozy comfort zones. It's not until we're stretched that we grow. Very little is accomplished on the couch, or even in the pew. We must get up, get moving, and chase that dream!

"For everyone to whom much is given, from him much
will be required; and to whom much has been committed, of
him they will ask the more."

Luke 12:48

Increased blessings also bring with them increased responsibilities, and to some people, responsibility is an even more terrifying pressure. If we do not understand this, the devil will beat us up with fear until we quit. We must pull on the undergirding strength of the Holy Spirit, tell the devil to take a hike, and carry out those responsibilities with godliness and wisdom. God expects profit and benefits from the blessings He gives us. We cannot expect the achievement of our dreams, much less an eternal reward, if we don't make use of everything He has given us to use.

In the parable of the talents, Jesus tells of three servants who received gifts from their master. The master departed for a while, and the first two servants used their talents and multiplied them, but the third servant did nothing with his. When the master returned, he was extremely pleased with the first two servants because his investment in them had proved profitable. But when he learned of the third servant's lack of industriousness, this was his response:

> *"But his lord answered and said to him, 'You wicked and lazy servant, you knew that I reap where I have not sown, and gather where I have not scattered seed.*
>
> *"'So you ought to have deposited my money with the bankers, and at my coming I would have received back my own with interest.*
>
> *"'Therefore take the talent from him, and give it to him who has ten talents.*
>
> *"'For to everyone who has, more will be given, and he will have abundance; but from him who does not have, even what he has will be taken away.*
>
> *"'And cast the unprofitable servant into the outer darkness. There will be weeping and gnashing of teeth.'"*
>
> Matthew 25:26-30

If we are blessed, we must ask ourselves, "What fruit can we present to justify God's investment in us?" If we are not profitable to God, if we do not take responsibility for the gifts and talents and financial abundance He has given us, then God has no reason to continue blessing us. Jesus cursed barren, unfruitful trees and declared that vines which do not yield fruit get pruned. (See Matthew 21:19 and John 15:1-2.) How much more will He judge us for not using all He has given us through His blood, His Word, and His name?

As we reach higher and higher levels of blessing, maturity, and responsibility, we must continue in the basics: Stay close to God, pray without ceasing, study the Word of God and apply it to our lives, love as He loves, and live as Jesus lived. This will keep us rising stronger and stronger, becoming tougher and tougher as soldiers for Christ! The key is to keep fighting and keep growing.

Contented Dissatisfaction

This will sound odd, but there is a healthy, godly tension between contentment and dissatisfaction that we can enjoy as children of God. Reaching a goal and achieving a God-given dream is one of the most fulfilling human experiences. No feeling in this world can equal the knowing in our hearts that we have pleased the Father. Yet, no matter what level of blessing we attain or what God-given dreams we achieve, we can always accomplish something more. We can always receive a deeper revelation of Him. We can be content inwardly, satisfied that we have pleased our Lord, and yet still desire to move on to greater heights of maturity in Him and mightier exploits for His glory.

First, let's examine contentment. The apostle Paul learned not to be concerned about material and natural things, but to be content inwardly:

> *Not that I speak in regard to need, for I have learned in whatever state I am, to be content:*
>
> *I know how to be abased, and I know how to abound. Everywhere and in all things I have learned both to be full and to be hungry, both to abound and to suffer need.*
>
> *I can do all things through Christ who strengthens me.*
>
> Philippians 4:11-13

Paul told the Corinthian church that when we walk with God according to His plan, temporary, physical things lose their importance compared to eternal things.

> *For our light affliction, which is but for a moment, is working for us a far more exceeding and eternal weight of glory,*
>
> *while we do not look at the things which are seen, but at the things which are not seen. For the things which are seen are temporary, but the things which are not seen are eternal.*
>
> 2 Corinthians 4:17-18

We can see from these scriptures that Paul had learned what it means to be content in whatever situation he found himself. However, other passages of Scripture also indicate there was a dissatisfaction within Paul when it came to his service to God and his maturity in God. Although he was satisfied in whatever physical condition in which he found himself, at the same time he also said, "I'm not satisfied." He was dissatisfied in a spiritual sense because there was always more to do and a continuous hunger for the deeper things of God. He always wanted to pursue godliness, to steadfastly seek the kingdom of God and His righteousness. As he achieved one God-given dream, he looked for another to pursue.

> *Yet indeed I also count all things loss for the excellence of the knowledge of Christ Jesus my Lord, for whom I have suffered the loss of all things, and count them as rubbish, that I may gain Christ*
>
> *and be found in Him, not having my own righteousness, which is from the law, but that which is through faith in Christ, the righteousness which is from God by faith;*
>
> *that I may know Him and the power of His resurrection, and the fellowship of His sufferings, being conformed to His death. . . .*
>
> *Brethren, I do not count myself to have apprehended; but one thing I do, forgetting those things which are behind and reaching forward to those things which are ahead,*
>
> *I press toward the goal for the prize of the upward call of God in Christ Jesus.*
>
> Philippians 3:8-10,13-14

When we can truly say with Paul that we are "content, but not satisfied," we are ready to handle any affliction on the road to our dreams. We have then become tough for God but are looking for opportunities to become tougher. When we are willing and prepared to endure any hardship, suffer any indignity, and weather any persecution, we can arrive at any dream God gives us. Demons will be defeated at every level, all He has bestowed upon us will be multiplied, and we will bring glory to His name!

Faith *for* Affliction

Chapter 7

en and Trisha had been Christians for a year, and they were growing in faith every day. Old things had truly passed away and all things had become new. They hungered for God's Word and drank deeply of the living water. Yet things weren't perfect with them. Ben still got his migraine headaches occasionally, and Trisha's family and coworkers still gave her a hard time about her new life in Christ.

When they asked for prayer for these ongoing problems, they found themselves receiving more and more criticism and less and less compassion. Church people told them that they didn't have enough faith. They needed to go to this meeting or that convention, then they'd be able to destroy the power of sin and unbelief in their lives that manifested as headaches and persecution.

A year later, after chasing miracles all over the country, Ben and Trisha found themselves still not healed or delivered and under tremendous condemnation from their church. Finally, they quit going to church and fell by the wayside, just two more victims of a twisted doctrine. The twisted doctrine to which I refer is that any affliction a believer experiences should be immediately eliminated by the exercise of their faith in God. It becomes even more twisted by those who believe that if you truly are walking in faith, no affliction at all can come upon you.

Some Christians believe and preach that if your affliction is not instantaneously, or at the most within a few days, completely erased from your life, then you are not walking in adequate faith or you are in sin. I have even heard some people say that saved folk who are strong in faith don't get sick, and if they do, God heals them right away. Likewise, they aren't poor, and if they are, God prospers them as soon as they start tithing and giving offerings.

Many Christians spend great time and effort developing faith to obtain healing, prosperity, and miracles, and there is nothing wrong with this! It is especially important if they come into the kingdom with tremendous needs that they seek the ways and Word of God to obtain all He has bought for them through the blood of Jesus Christ. All of us want to be healthy, wealthy, and supernaturally strong. But we must not become so obsessed with these things that we forget the service of God and holy living. We must not seek the hand of God so much that we forget to seek His face. The balance that must be struck is this: We are saved, healed, delivered, and set free for one purpose—not to please ourselves, but to serve God.

Who Is Serving Whom?

I see something devastating happening in the American church in particular. We ignore the lessons in the life of Joseph, a life in which we see a faithful believer enduring great obstacles and persecution on his way to his God-given dreams. Too many of us have become so excited about getting what we want that we forget about doing God's will and working for God's kingdom. We go to God with our shopping list of requests, with our agenda and expectations. Either we have never been taught or we forget that we are there to ask, "Lord, what do You want me to do for You?" Our lives are hid in God, and it is our obligation and privilege to inquire of Him, "What is *Your* plan for my life?"

Consider this illustration. It would be very unwise for an employee to come to his boss with such an urgent list of demands and requests that he rattled on and on about them and gave the boss no opportunity to tell him what he was supposed to do. You think that's crazy, but we do it to God all the time. If we are servants of the Most High God, we could say we are His employees and He is our employer. Are we more concerned about His will for us and His plan for our lives than we are about cramming our agenda down His throat in "prayer"?

How would you like it, for example, if your child came to you one evening and said, "Okay, dear Mom, tomorrow I want a banana split for breakfast. Then I'm going to skip school and go to the water park. That's the plan, Mom. I know you can make it happen. Oh, and I'm sorry I busted that lamp and shaved the cat again. Thanks for forgiving me. I love you, Mom. You're the greatest. You're my mom! Oh, and I want an extra-large pizza for lunch and two for dinner, and tomorrow we're going to the toy store so you can buy me everything I want. I have faith in you, Mom! Amen."

In real life, you'd wear that child out, wouldn't you? Yet we very nearly do that to God and think nothing of it. We expect Him to bless our greedy, shortsighted little plans and never bother to find out what wonderful things *He* has planned for our lives. Then we wonder why our prayers go unanswered! We become frustrated and miserable without a clue as to why.

What Is Your Obsession?

If you are obsessed with anything or anyone else other than Jesus Christ, you will get into trouble. If you go through the motions of serving Him for personal gain, you will be deceived and ultimately defeated in life.

Many believers have become so obsessed with miracles and blessings that they lose compassion for others who are struggling. They condemn those who are not healed or do not prosper right away. If we believe that no Christian is ever supposed to be sick, we also must believe that something is wrong with a believer's faith or character if they do get sick.

This obsession with the supernatural is dangerous because it gives rise to all kinds of deceptions and abuses. Many people have died after being told they were healed and should cease taking medicine. Many have left good Bible-teaching churches to run around the world following ministers who dangled before them the promise of miracles and healing. As the extreme of this particular false teaching has traveled through the body of Christ, many believers have adopted the mindset that if they're facing adversity, they must have faltered in their faith, sinned, or missed God.

> *"For false christs and false prophets will rise and show great signs and wonders to deceive, if possible, even the elect."*
>
> Matthew 24:24

Of course, a believer can open the door to the devil by willful rebellion; God does heal so that medicine is no longer needed; and God does raise up ministers who are anointed to heal the sick. So how do we know the difference between the real and the counterfeit? How do we know what is really going on in our lives? The only way to keep it straight is to stay focused on God's Word and walk in His Spirit.

Believers get into deception and error when they begin looking for something new and spectacular and take their eyes off God's Word. They go to this meeting and that meeting to get the latest prophecies, the new revelations, and to see signs, wonders, and miracles when the truth of God's Word, properly applied, would meet their every need.

If Christians would study their Bible for themselves and pray and ask the Holy Spirit to speak to them, they would see clearly that good, faithful believers do see affliction. They would also see that they have been given everything they need to overcome it. Moreover, they can view affliction from God's eternal perspective. Paul spoke about this in his second letter to the Corinthians:

> *Therefore we do not lose heart. Even though our outward man is perishing, yet the inward man is being renewed day by day.*
>
> *For our light affliction, which is but for a moment, is working for us a far more exceeding and eternal weight of glory,*
>
> *while we do not look at the things which are seen, but at the things which are not seen. For the things which are seen are temporary, but the things which are not seen are eternal.*

We are saved, healed,
delivered, and set free
for one purpose——
not to please ourselves,
but to serve God.

For we know that if our earthly house, this tent, is destroyed, we have a building from God, a house not made with hands, eternal in the heavens.

2 Corinthians 4:16-5:1

This may run counter to popular teaching, but Jesus is not primarily concerned with our attainment of money, health, and earthly provisions. His concern is that we be saved from sin and serve Him before anyone or anything else. He knows that when we seek first His kingdom, His face, His will, and His Word, all these other things and blessings will come upon us. Why? So we can serve Him even better!

There can be no doubt that we can serve the Lord better if we are not continuously sick, mentally tormented, and scrounging to obtain our next meal. That's why Jesus came to set the captives free! And when we seek His kingdom before anything else, serving Him with whatever we have and in whatever situation in which we find ourselves, we begin our walk to freedom. Even if we're bedfast, we can pray. No matter how poor we are, we can find *something* to put in the offering. We can take the time to help in the Sunday school class. Then, as we are faithful and continue to seek God first, all these things—health, wealth, and well-being—will be added to us. They will grow in our lives, and we will have more and more of His ability working in us to achieve His dreams.

Contentment, joy, peace, and all we need for our natural lives are ours if we put God first. On the other hand, if we seek the "other things" before God, our lives will be upside down and our dreams cannot be realized.

Jesus answered them and said, "Most assuredly, I say to you, you seek Me, not because you saw the signs, but because you ate of the loaves and were filled.

"Do not labor for the food which perishes, but for the food which endures to everlasting life, which the Son of Man will give you. . . ."

And Jesus said to them, "I am the bread of life. He who comes to Me shall never hunger, and he who believes in Me shall never thirst."

John 6:26-27,35

Afflictions come because we live in a sin-driven, Satan-commanded, demon-infested world; but the good news is that Jesus has overcome the world! When we are obsessed with Him — with His Word, the power of His Spirit, His precious blood — we have the grace and wisdom to walk through fire and flood and come out victoriously on the other side. When we seek Him first, we are true witnesses of the Gospel.

And my speech and my preaching were not with persuasive words of human wisdom, but in demonstration of the Spirit and of power,

that your faith should not be in the wisdom of men but in the power of God.

1 Corinthians 2:4-5

Affliction Cometh

You will be sadly disappointed if you believe every Christian who has faith will reach their God-given dreams without trouble

Tough times are usually
not caused by a lack of faith
but by the very faith with
which we are choosing
to follow God.

or distress. A believer who feels that life is always going to be beautiful and that they will overcome every form of opposition without effort is destined to be defeated. The Word of God makes it all too clear that we will suffer persecution for the Gospel's sake:

> *Yes, and all who desire to live godly in Christ Jesus will suffer persecution.*
>
> 2 Timothy 3:12

> *"We must through many tribulations enter the kingdom of God."*
>
> Acts 14:22

> *Beloved, do not think it strange concerning the fiery trial which is to try you, as though some strange thing happened to you.*
>
> 1 Peter 4:12

What we won't find in Scripture is a basis for the assertion that everyone who accepts Jesus as Lord and Savior is going to be spared from trouble and affliction. It simply isn't there, and those who preach otherwise are wrong. The life of the apostle Paul also bears this out.

> *Of the Jews five times received I forty stripes save one.*
>
> *Thrice was I beaten with rods, once was I stoned, thrice I suffered shipwreck, a night and a day I have been in the deep;*
>
> *In journeyings often, in perils of waters, in perils of robbers, in perils by mine own countrymen, in perils by the*

heathen, in perils in the city, in perils in the wilderness, in perils in the sea, in perils among false brethren;

In weariness and painfulness, in watchings often, in hunger and thirst, in fastings often, in cold and nakedness.

2 Corinthians 11:24-27 KJV

Not only will we be persecuted for the Gospel's sake if we obey God and pursue our dreams, but we can expect the devil to try to come in and wreak havoc through any weakness we have. If we have a specific fear or worry, there will be a demon assigned to make certain that thing will paralyze us. And everyone has physical challenges throughout their lives. The early church was no exception. Paul speaks of Timothy's stomach problems in 1 Timothy 5:23. He had to leave his evangelistic team member, Trophimus, sick at the town of Miletus, as described in 2 Timothy 4:20. Another team member, Epaphroditus, had been struck by an extended serious illness, almost unto death, from which he recovered only after a period of time. (See Philippians 2:25-27.) Paul was not surprised by afflictions.

You know that because of physical infirmity I preached the gospel to you at the first.

And my trial which was in my flesh you did not despise or reject, but you received me as an angel of God, even as Christ Jesus.

Galatians 4:13-14

Notice how Paul commends the Galatians for not despising him or the Gospel he preached because he had a physical infirmity at the time he presented it to them. Today, many believers would not attend a minister's meeting if they knew that minister was fighting an illness. They need to read their Bibles!

Paul also knew that these types of afflictions are enemies to God and enemies to His servants. Sickness, disease, and death are in opposition to God and painful to us. They did not originate with Him, but came as a result of man's disobedience to Him. The entrance of sin into the experience of humanity caused illness and death.

> *Therefore, just as through one man sin entered the world, and death through sin, and thus death spread to all men, because all sinned.*

> Romans 5:12

The Bible lets us know that God created a world in which there was no sickness or death. The universe was one vast symphony in which God and man played beautiful music together. Our disobedience and sin spoiled that. Make no mistake! Despite what popular culture says, God does not kill us or take our loved ones away. God does not make us sick. He does not birth us into poverty and dysfunctional families. Satan and sin are the culprits, so stop slamming God for sickness and death! He hates them more than we do. He hates them so much, He sent Jesus to die so that we could be free of them.

> *But God demonstrates his own love toward us, in that while we were still sinners, Christ died for us.*

Much more then, having now been justified by His blood,
we shall be saved from wrath through Him.

Romans 5:8-9

Jesus has already prevailed. Satan, death, sickness, and the grave have already been tried, found guilty, and sentenced. They are on death row now, and in awhile they will be summoned for execution. We know this because we've read the end of the Book:

The devil, who deceived them, was cast into the lake of fire
and brimstone where the beast and the false prophet are. And
they will be tormented day and night forever and ever.

Revelation 20:10

Then Death and Hades were cast into the lake of fire. This
is the second death.

Revelation 20:14

Ultimately, sickness, sin, and death have no hold on us because of the atoning blood of Jesus. Their authority over us has been broken, and one day they will no longer exist. God will wipe away every tear. Here is His Word on it:

"O Death, where is your sting?
O Hades, where is your victory?"

The sting of death is sin, and the strength of sin is the law.

But thanks be to God, who gives us the victory through
our Lord Jesus Christ.

1 Corinthians 15:55-57

"And God will wipe away every tear from their eyes; there shall be no more death, nor sorrow, nor crying. There shall be no more pain, for the former things have passed away."

Revelation 21:4

In the meantime, times may be mean. If you have not had a time that was mean, you will. Sickness is a "mean time." Death is a "mean time." Economic trouble is a "mean time." Life has those "mean times." Let us not be surprised by the afflictions that come our way. Just as Joseph's path to the palace was filled with pits and prisons, our path through God's plan will also include afflictions. Don't let anyone tell you any differently. To achieve our God-given dreams, to accomplish God's great plan for our lives, we need to decide that no "mean time," no affliction, is going to stop us from serving and loving God.

Seeking His Will

Now after reading the last few pages, some may accuse me of preaching unbelief, of advocating sickness and poverty and torment. They might say that I should only be preaching healing and deliverance because if I did that, people would never be sick or afflicted. Well, I *do* preach healing and deliverance. I believe in miracles. I have received many healings and miracles myself, and I have seen others receive them through my ministry. But I also preach a holy God who has only one basic requirement of us: to serve Him only. He wants our whole heart and our whole life. The purpose of miracles and healing and deliverance is to set the captives free *to serve Him.*

"Heal the sick, cleanse the lepers, raise the dead, cast out demons. Freely you have received, freely give."

Matthew 10:8

Make no mistake about it; God is a God of miracles. His Word promises us great blessings. The Bible promises in Ephesians 6:1-3 that children who obey their parents will live long on the earth. Jesus states in Matthew 17:20 that we'll have the power to move mountains. Proverbs 22:6 promises that if we train up children in the way they should go, when they are old, they will not depart. These and many more scriptures tell us that God's power is available to believers.

Strong biblical faith consistently eradicates whole categories of illnesses such as psychologically induced sicknesses, dysfunctional emotional responses, and demonic intrusions. And then, even in the case of actual material and physical malfunctions, God sometimes breaks in and miraculously shows Himself to be God. He gets glory, He convinces men of His power, and He fulfills His purpose. He demonstrates His love by performing signs, wonders, and miracles. There are times, places, and people upon which He will place a strong anointing so that His power is greatly manifested. When He does, we should get in on the move of God and ride the wave of His power.

Nevertheless, having said that, I must point out that even those who get their healing or their miracle may not get it right away. During that waiting period they will need to know how to live through it. Still others will need to know how to live through their affliction because the waiting period may be a long one. These precious saints will need the grace of God and the encouragement and prayers of other believers to overcome the afflictions they are facing. And some of what they're facing is the timing of God. The Bible says we inherit the promises through faith *and patience.* (See Hebrews 6:12.)

Knowing God's Timing

Our faith cannot override God's ultimate plan. We cannot change God's schedule of events, nor should we try to. We should always ask and believe according to His Word and the guidance of His Spirit, but we must also leave the timing and methods up to God. When He does not do what we ask Him to do, we must not lose faith! He has His reasons, and the Bible says He will bring all hidden things to light. (See 1 Corinthians 4:5.) He is God and we can trust Him. The important thing to remember is that we are here to seek His will and to do it, no matter what is going on in our lives.

> *You do not know what will happen tomorrow. For what is your life? It is even a vapor that appears for a little time and then vanishes away.*
>
> *Instead you ought to say, "If the Lord wills, we shall live and do this or that."*

James 4:14-15

Persevering faith trusts God no matter what happens. Sometimes God opens up heaven and pours out blessings and everything is wonderful. But sometimes the way becomes rough. Our hearts get heavy, yet we still must trust God's plan for our lives. He knows the perfect time for all things to come to pass.

*For this reason I also suffer these things; nevertheless I am
not ashamed, for I know whom I have believed and am
persuaded that He is able to keep what I have committed to
Him until that Day.*

2 Timothy 1:12

God has wonderful plans for us, and I believe that when I go
to God and tell Him what I want and how I want it, I just might
be shortchanging myself. He has far more in store for me than I
can imagine. Did I imagine thirty years ago that I would be
called by the Lord to be a leader in my denomination? Of course
not! I simply asked to be used in God's plan. I humbly obeyed
and worked hard at each task He sent my way. I never asked the
Lord to work my agenda; I only asked if I could work His
agenda. I just prayed and obeyed.

I can't say this enough. We must not try to force our agendas
on the Lord because what we think is good for us may not be
good for us. What's more, everything that is good *to* us may not
be good *for* us. We need to let God plan the menu because He is
able to do exceedingly abundantly above all that we ask or think.
(See Ephesians 3:20.) Above all, we must trust Him to see us
through any affliction that comes our way, knowing that He is
the author and the finisher of our faith. What He has promised,
He will do.

God sees our adversaries and our afflictions differently from
the way we do. He sees the end from the beginning. He sees the
big picture. Tough times are usually not caused by a lack of faith
but by the very faith with which we are choosing to follow God.
Although the devil intends for those afflictions to destroy us,

they will only serve to strengthen our resolve, to give glory to God, and to refine us into greater purity. Truly, when we exert our faith through all affliction, what Satan has meant for evil turns to our good and the good of all whom we touch in the name of Jesus.

Just remember the old mule who endured his affliction in the well by stepping up onto all the trash and garbage that was thrown on him. If a mule can figure out what to do with affliction, certainly blood-bought, Spirit-filled, Word-believing Christians can. And when we do, there is no stopping the manifestation of our dreams!

Getting Unlocked

Have you ever felt like you were locked in a pattern of failure and defeat? Joseph may have felt that way when he became a slave in Potiphar's household, and again when he was thrown into Pharaoh's prison. But each time, he made the quality decision to trust God to break this pattern of destruction in his life. He made maximum use of all his assets and was able to break out of situations when others stayed locked in. I can't help but wonder if he didn't set a standard that others have used through the centuries to break out of their locked-in situations.

With this in mind, let's look at the story of Esther, a woman who found herself locked into a terrible situation yet still managed to perform the role God ordained for her. Esther is a powerful role model for anyone today who feels they can never reach for their God-given dreams because they are locked into their position and freedom seems impossible to obtain.

Locked in the Palace

So it was, when the king's command and decree were heard, and when many young women were gathered at

Shushan the citadel, under the custody of Hegai, that Esther also was taken to the king's palace, into the care of Hegai the custodian of the women.

Now the young woman pleased him, and she obtained his favor; so he readily gave beauty preparations to her, besides her allowance. Then seven choice maidservants were provided for her from the king's palace, and he moved her and her maidservants to the best place in the house of the women.

Esther had not revealed her people or family, for Mordecai had charged her not to reveal it. . . .

Now when the turn came for Esther the daughter of Abihail the uncle of Mordecai, who had taken her as his daughter, to go in to the king, she requested nothing but what Hegai the king's eunuch, the custodian of the women, advised. And Esther obtained favor in the sight of all who saw her.

So Esther was taken to King Ahasuerus, into his royal palace, in the tenth month, which is the month of Tebeth, in the seventh year of his reign.

The king loved Esther more than all the other women, and she obtained grace and favor in his sight more than all the virgins; so he set the royal crown upon her head and made her queen instead of Vashti.

Esther 2:8-10,15-17

Ahasuerus, also known as Xerxes, was the king of Persia, which was then the ruling power of the world. His kingdom covered over half of the known world. It was divided into 127 provinces and stretched from India to Ethiopia. The center of his empire was the citadel of Shushan where his throne and his palace were located.

To celebrate his stature and his accomplishments, Ahasuerus arranged an extravagant festival in Shushan. He invited his officials, his assistants, and all the nobles and princes of each of the provinces. For six months, all the wealth and splendor of his kingdom were displayed. At the same time his wife, Queen Vashti, hosted a feast for the women of the palace and the wives of those being entertained by the king. Eastern society did not allow women to be in the presence of men at these celebrations or even in the normal course of events. The women were to be veiled at all times when in public and could appear unveiled only before their husbands and close family members. Only concubines, singing girls, and women for pleasure were present when the men were intoxicated and involved in riotous occasions of this nature.

At such a time King Ahasuerus, probably drunk himself, called for his wife that he might display her, as he had displayed all his material possessions. He wanted his drunken crew to gape at the unveiled beauty of the first lady of his kingdom, the queen, the highest example of femininity and womanhood. When his servants went to fetch Vashti at his command, she refused to present herself. If she obeyed her king, she would disregard convention and the dignity and nobility of her person and position. Sometimes it's better to be alone and noble than to be with somebody who treats you like a doormat.

Because of Vashti's refusal, the counselors to the king recommended that he remove her and select another queen. Otherwise, they reasoned, all the wives in the kingdom would feel that they should also disobey their husbands. The Persians were not believers in Yahweh, nor did they adhere to His just laws. Thus Vashti was removed as queen and banished.

When the search for a new queen was launched, one of the many young women who were gathered into Shushan according to the decree of the king was a Jewish girl named Esther. Her Jewish name was Hadassah. Orphaned as a child, she had been adopted by her older cousin Mordecai, a Benjamite Jew.

It seems to me that Esther's presence in the palace was not something over which either Mordecai or Esther had any control. Esther and the other young ladies were placed under the supervision of Hegai, the king's servant, for one year of cleansing and preparation. What were Esther and the other young women preparing for? Each would spend one night with the king. After that night they would be carried to the second house of the women, never to see the king again unless he called for them by name.

Esther was terribly locked in! As a powerless subject in a despotic dictatorship, she became locked into the system, destined to spend her life confined in a house of women after being used for a one-night fling. The possibility of her ever being free, ever marrying anyone else, or ever becoming queen was extremely remote. This nice Jewish girl became one of the women of a king to whom only one of them would be married, and their only way out would be to die.

Today we may not be locked into a king's palace, forced to be his concubine or slave, but there are other ways of being locked in. A physical or emotional handicap can lock us in. A

Many of our loved ones
are locked into poverty
and drug abuse. But
locks can be picked . . .

life-threatening event over which we had no control can lock us in. An educational deficiency can lock us in. Our color or our race can lock us in. Our appearance can lock us in. Our profession or job can lock us in. A marital choice can lock us in. A sexual fling can lock us in. There are a thousand ways to be locked in. Some things affect us for life. But no matter how bad they are, are they really reasons for us to give up on our God-given dreams?

Esther was locked in, but she did not lose it, go off, or surrender to despair. Like Joseph, she made the best of a terrible situation. She maximized her emotional and personal beauty. We're not really beautiful until our words are beautiful, until our thoughts are beautiful, until our attitudes toward people and life are beautiful. Just because we are in a bad situation does not mean we have to have a defeated attitude that results in failure. Failure is often a choice we make when the struggle gets too hard.

I wish I had room to write about all the people in the Bible who were locked in. Daniel was locked in the lions' den; Shadrach, Meshach, and Abednego were locked into the fiery furnace; and they were all locked into slavery in Babylon. Joseph was locked into slavery and prison. Our black forebears were locked into slavery and oppression. Many of our loved ones are locked into poverty and drug abuse.

But locks can be picked . . .

Breaking Out

Esther chose to have an overcoming attitude, and because of her attitude, Hegai held her in high esteem. In addition to what he gave to everyone else, he gave Esther beauty preparations, seven maids from the king's palace, and then moved her and her maids to the best place in the house of women. (See Esther 2:8-9.)

In an effort to make the best of her situation, Esther sought and submitted to wise advice. She stayed in contact with Mordecai and followed his every instruction, and God blessed her for it. This is a very important point because some folk will not listen to anybody. Others will listen, but they wait until it's too late, or they listen to the wrong people. This is why we have pastors and those in the Church who are authorized to teach and counsel. A word of warning here, though. Watch out for those self-appointed counselors and teachers and stick to those whom God has obviously appointed and anointed. Study the fruit of their lives and always compare their advice to God's Word, which is a lamp to your feet and a light to your path. (See Psalm 119:105.) Pray for a discerning heart.

> *"And I will give you shepherds* [pastors and those appointed by the pastor] *according to My heart, who will feed you with knowledge and understanding."*
>
> Jeremiah 3:15 (insert mine)

When Mordecai advised Esther not to reveal that she was a Jew, she obeyed him because she knew of his godly wisdom and love for her. Furthermore, she requested nothing but what Hegai, the king's eunuch and custodian of the women, advised because she recognized his skill and knowledge in palace matters. (See Esther 2:15.) Then she was patient. For twelve months, all she did was get ready and wait. This may be the hardest part of breaking out of our situations. God works on His timetable, not ours. He's never too early and He's never too late. If we act under our own wisdom, we're likely to jump the gun or drag our feet. Only God's timing is perfect.

> *Have you not known?*
> *Have you not heard?*
> *The everlasting God, the* LORD,
> *The Creator of the ends of the earth,*
> *Neither faints nor is weary.*
> *His understanding is unsearchable.*
>
> *He gives power to the weak,*
> *And to those who have no might He increases strength.*
>
> *Even the youths shall faint and be weary,*
> *And the young men shall utterly fall,*
>
> *But those who wait on the* LORD
> *Shall renew their strength;*
> *They shall mount up with wings like eagles,*
> *They shall run and not be weary,*
> *They shall walk and not faint.*

Isaiah 40:28-31

To break out, we must go through periods of waiting on the Lord. This isn't just sitting around doing nothing and twiddling our thumbs. The Hebrew word for "wait" means to bind ourselves to the Lord.[1] God wants us to spend this time connecting with Him and becoming intimate with Him. We must keep

---

[1] *Strong's Exhaustive Concordance of the Bible,* "Hebrew and Chaldee Dictionary," by J. B. Strong (Atlanta: Thomas Nelson Publishers, 1990), #6960, p. 102.

our eyes on His Word and His counsel rather than on the worldly advice and distractions of those around us. Thus we gain the strength and courage we will need when God finally releases us from our locked-in condition to the realization of our God-given dream.

During this time of testing, preparation, and patience, there will be times when it seems that all we are doing is getting ready and waiting . . . and waiting . . . and waiting. It may seem that life is saying, "Hurry up and wait." This is when we bind ourselves to God, knowing that it is going to happen in His time, not ours. Waiting on the Lord paid off for Esther:

> *Now when the turn came for Esther the daughter of Abihail the uncle of Mordecai, who had taken her as his daughter, to go in to the king, she requested nothing but what Hegai the king's eunuch, the custodian of the women, advised. And Esther obtained favor in the sight of all who saw her.*

> Esther 2:15

From this verse we can notice first that there was an economy about Esther. She was not extravagant, immoderate, capricious, wasteful, or reckless. She could have gone in to the king painted up to look like a peacock and strutting like a turkey. But she wisely took the advice of Hegai and did all he counseled her to do.

Esther had self-control. She was not driven by pride, desperation, or emotional hunger. She was not driven by insecurity, which is simply fear. When we long to break free of our situation, emotional fear and hunger are dangerous and destructive.

They handicap some people to be completely "into themselves" rather than having concern for others. Some people are vogue on the outside and vague on the inside. It is important to dress up the heart and mind on the inside and then to dress up the outside appropriately. There is a beauty about economy, simplicity, and self-control—and Esther was beautiful for all these reasons.

Notice also that Esther did not have a "gimmie" mentality. She was obviously a very generous, giving person. The verse says, **And Esther obtained favor in the sight of all who saw her.** The Bible teaches that a beautiful woman or a handsome man won't gain favor just because they look good. They have to be warm, interested in people, and show concern for their needs and preferences. Any human being who behaves this way toward others will see God reward their generosity with favor, just as He rewarded Esther.

> *"Give, and it will be given to you: good measure, pressed down, shaken together, and running over will be put into your bosom. For with the same measure that you use, it will be measured back to you."*

> Luke 6:38

When Esther was trying to break free from her situation, we also notice she sought wisdom, not things. The same was true with Joseph. The more he learned about his situation, the better he was able to perform well and be rewarded. And we have another astounding example of a believer's quest for wisdom in Solomon. As a young man suddenly made king of Israel, he asked God only for wisdom:

"Now give me wisdom and knowledge, that I may go out and come in before this people; for who can judge this great people of Yours?"

Then God said to Solomon: "Because this was in your heart, and you have not asked riches or wealth or honor or the life of your enemies, nor have you asked long life – but have asked wisdom and knowledge for yourself, that you may judge My people over whom I have made you king –

"wisdom and knowledge are granted to you."

2 Chronicles 1:10-12

Although he is known as the wisest man and one of the wealthiest men who has ever lived, Solomon did not always put God first, as both Joseph and Esther did. Through their entire lives, Joseph and Esther only wanted what God wanted in their lives. They walked with Him with all their hearts. The rest of Esther's story is much like Joseph's because she lived by the same principles Joseph lived by. Esther began to break out of her locked-in situation when she became Ahasuerus' queen. But her complete freedom came only after she risked everything to save her Jewish people from destruction. All that preparation and waiting on the Lord gave her the wisdom and the courage to do what she was called to do. In the end, Queen Esther triumphed and brought glory to her people and her king. However, she would not have succeeded had she not been willing to change her ways; to improve herself in spirit, soul, and body; and to get rid of anything that would hinder God's dream coming to pass in her life.

If we were to unburden
ourselves of anything
that God does not want us
carrying, we might find
ourselves light enough to fly
over the walls of the prison
we've made for ourselves.

Dump Day

I wonder what would happen if God's people would say to Him, "What You want we want, and we don't want anything that You don't want us to have." The result would be that situations we thought we were locked into would become springboards to our greatest successes. Our lowest moments would give way to our highest achievements. If we were to unburden ourselves of anything that God does not want us carrying, we might find ourselves light enough to fly over the walls of the prison we've made for ourselves.

> *Let us lay aside every weight, and the sin which so easily ensnares us, and let us run with endurance the race that is set before us,*
>
> *looking unto Jesus, the author and finisher of our faith, who for the joy that was set before Him endured the cross, despising the shame, and has sat down at the right hand of the throne of God.*

Hebrews 12:1-2

Several years ago the staff of our church, West Angeles Church of God in Christ, was confronted by a significant problem. We had accumulated so many documents—letters, old bills, records, memos, financial documents, forms, and almost every other kind of document—that our organization was almost paralyzed. We had run out of storage space. Desks and file cabinets were filled and overflowing. Table and cabinet tops had stacks of paper piled on top of them. So many unnecessary documents took up space that we had trouble finding the documents we really needed. This jeopardized progress and effectiveness. To deal with this situation, I announced what is now a periodic institution within our organization: Dump Day.

On Dump Day, we usually close the office to the public, put volunteers on the phone lines, request that the staff cancel all outside appointments, and we dress in old clothes and tennis shoes. We order extra trash bins, paper shredders, and large plastic bags, and we dump or throw away hundreds if not thousands of pounds of paper, empty ballpoint pens, antiquated and broken equipment, and everything else that might hinder us from reaching a higher level of effectiveness as an organization. We have found out that "stuff" routinely piles up on us, but it does not routinely get dumped. Therefore, from time to time, we have to call everything else to a halt and have a Dump Day. Our motto for the day is, "When in doubt, dump it."

On a recent Dump Day, as I was stepping over a huge pile of paper I had removed from my desk, I was strongly impressed—I believe by the Lord—that Dump Days should be instituted by many organizations, groups, households, and individuals. Some folk need to have a Dump Day for their yards. Say good-bye to old cars that will never run again, old chairs that will injure you if you try to sit in them, old couches that stray dogs and cats have been sleeping on. Have a Dump Day for the yard.

Other folk need a Dump Day for the inside of their houses. In fact, let's talk about your closet. You've got stuff in there that you have not worn in ten years. Dump it! Outfits from the sixties, thick-soled shoes, bell-bottom pants, and other stuff that belongs in a museum. Dump it! You've got stuff that you haven't been able to wedge yourself into since you were twenty-five, and if you actually got in them, paramedics would have to come and cut you out! You've got stuff in there that, if you wore it, folk would know that you are way older than you say you are, so dump it!

What about the kitchen? If you open a box and it's moving, dump it. That flour and meal that you bought five years ago, knowing you don't make anything from scratch, needs to go. If the top of the can is rusty and dusty, dump it. If scientists come to your refrigerator to study the growth of strange new life forms, dump it!

If there is so much junk in the house that you feel you're wading instead of walking, then you need to have a Dump Day. Old magazines, newspapers, and catalogs that you'll never read again or that you never read in the first place should be dumped!

Some old folk need to have a Dump Day because they are living in the past. Some young folk need to have a Dump Day because they are loaded down with foolish stuff. White folk, black folk, men, women, those in between, Democrats, Republicans, whatever group you may name; there is a universal need to occasionally have a Dump Day.

Now let's focus on the individual who desires to reach their God-given dreams, but they are locked in to destructive patterns of thinking and behavior. As Christians, we all need to have regular Dump Days! There are plenty of things in our minds, our souls, our spirits, and our relationships that need to be dumped because they prevent us from moving closer to God and reaching for our dreams.

I'm reminded of the Asian monkey trap that is nothing more than a heavy pot with a narrow neck. A peanut is placed inside the pot to lure the monkey. The monkey's hand can reach into the pot, but when he grabs the peanut, his fist becomes too big to come back out. The pot is too big to carry away, so the monkey is stuck unless he dumps the peanut. Most monkeys are too hard-headed to let go, and they stay trapped.

Before we laugh at the stupid monkey, think of the things which trap us because we won't let go! To attain our God-given dreams, we need to let go and lay aside every weight, and the sin which so easily ensnares us. Why? So we can run with endurance the race that is set before us. (See Hebrews 12:1.) Someone who runs with a backpack full of rocks is at a disadvantage to a runner who has laid aside every weight. Yet we voluntarily try to run toward our dreams with a load of stuff that's holding us back and slowing us down. Dump it!

> *Do you not know that those who run in a race all run, but one receives the prize? Run in such a way that you may obtain it.*
>
> *And everyone who competes for the prize is temperate in all things. Now they do it to obtain a perishable crown, but we for an imperishable crown.*
>
> *Therefore I run thus: not with uncertainty. Thus I fight: not as one who beats the air.*
>
> *But I discipline my body and bring it into subjection, lest, when I have preached to others, I myself should become disqualified.*
>
> 1 Corinthians 9:24-27

There are things that we must lay aside if we are to run well in this race. The more we lay aside, the better we run. In a race, the runners wear very light clothing and shoes. They carry nothing that is not absolutely necessary. So many people go through life carrying unnecessary and incapacitating burdens.

Now be careful at this point because you'll find some things are necessary. In a relay race, the runner must run with a baton, which he passes to the next runner. If he drops it, or does not pick it up, his whole team loses. Paul ran his race loaded with the Gospel of grace. It was certainly a burden at times, but he knew that reaching the lost with the Gospel *was* his race, so he held on to it with all his might.

> *"But none of these things move me; nor do I count my life dear to myself, so that I may finish my race with joy, and the ministry which I received from the Lord Jesus, to testify to the gospel of the grace of God."*
>
> Acts 20:24

In life's race we are sometimes inclined to hold on to what we don't need and throw away necessary things. Once when I was traveling, I changed planes in Dallas-Fort Worth International Airport. As I went through the airport, I noticed that my coat pocket was filled with empty ticket folders and various documents. In the spirit of Dump Day, I stopped by a trash can and unloaded. I was careful not to throw away my current plane ticket, but after my plane had taken off, I noticed a rather large check that had been in my pocket was gone. I realized that I had thrown it in the trash can at the airport. Fortunately, I was able to get a replacement check and stop payment on the discarded check, but I should have been more careful.

How do we know what to dump and what to keep? The Word of God tells us! Paul says in his letter to the church at Philippi:

> But what things were gain to me, these I have counted loss for Christ.
>
> Yet indeed I also count all things loss for the excellence of the knowledge of Christ Jesus my LORD, for whom I have suffered the loss of all things, and count them as rubbish, that I may gain Christ
>
> and be found in Him, not having my own righteousness, which is from the law, but that which is through faith in Christ, the righteousness which is from God by faith;
>
> that I may know Him and the power of His resurrection, and the fellowship of His sufferings, being conformed to His death.
>
> Philippians 3:7-10

We must hold on to Jesus Christ, value and cherish His righteousness which is given to us by faith, and know Him in the power of His resurrection and in the fellowship of His sufferings.

> Receive with meekness the implanted word, which is able to save your souls.
>
> James 1:21

To run our race, to reach our dreams, we must **pursue peace with all people, and holiness, without which no one will see** the Lord (Hebrews 12:14). We must turn away from our former ugly ways and **cleanse ourselves from all filthiness of the flesh and spirit, perfecting holiness in the fear of God** (2 Corinthians 7:1). And we will truly unburden ourselves when we shrug off our load of sin, when we **put off all these: anger, wrath, malice, blasphemy, filthy language out of your mouth** (Colossians 3:8).

We have no excuse because

> *The night is far spent, the day is at hand. Therefore let us cast off the works of darkness, and let us put on the armor of light.*
>
> *Let us walk properly, as in the day, not in revelry and drunkenness, not in lewdness and lust, not in strife and envy.*
>
> *But put on the Lord Jesus Christ, and make no provision for the flesh, to fulfill its lusts.*
>
> Romans 13:12-14

We must take off the old man of sin and put on Jesus Christ.

I shouldn't have to say this, but there are Christians who are still carrying loads from their old life before they were saved. Make no mistake, drunkenness is a sin. Alcohol and drugs are devastating our society and our world. How many of our young people have to be destroyed, how many careers have to be destroyed, how many families have to be ruined before people understand that they need to dump alcohol and drugs? Dump it!

Sexual immorality is a sin, no matter what our culture insists. *That means no sex outside of marriage,* period. Illegitimate children, disease, sorrow, and the judgment of God are the fruits of society's perversion of God's design for sex within marriage. We will not attain God's plan for our lives playing with sexual immorality. Dump it!

Hidden Weights

Every *weight* is not a sin, but a weight can lead to sin or weaken us so that we will be susceptible to sin. A weight is anything that can hinder us in the Christian race. People can be weights. When we hang out with the wrong kind of people, they can hold us back and drag us down. Our mamas were right about that, weren't they?

> For we have spent enough of our past lifetime in doing the will of the Gentiles — when we walked in lewdness, lusts, drunkenness, revelries, drinking parties, and abominable idolatries.
>
> In regard to these, they think it strange that you do not run with them in the same flood of dissipation, speaking evil of you.
>
> They will give an account to Him who is ready to judge the living and the dead.
>
> 1 Peter 4:3-5

We can't be saved and run with everybody, and we sure can't be successful and run with everybody. **Can two walk together, unless they are agreed** (Amos 3:3)? Are we lifting them up or are they bringing us down? If we're honest with ourselves, some of these folk have got to go—and stay gone.

As we unburden ourselves for the race toward our dreams, we realize how important our mental state is. We realize that we can't fill our minds full of the garbage on day-time or prime-time television. We cannot attend movies which depict ungodly beliefs and behavior we are seeking to dump from our lives. To win the race and get unlocked, we have to keep our sights higher and keep our hearts pure.

> *Whatever things are true, whatever things are noble, whatever things are just, whatever things are pure, whatever things are lovely, whatever things are of good report, if there is any virtue and if there is anything praiseworthy – meditate on these things.*

> Philippians 4:8

Some people are so negative that they won't let us think on the things we should. Their every word reflects the fact that their dreams are dead and they want to kill ours too. Avoid dream-killing people. If they're family and we're stuck with them, at least we can evict them from our meditation and our minds so we can think on what we should. Like the old Johnny Mercer song says, "Accentuate the positive, eliminate the negative."

> *Be anxious for nothing, but in everything by prayer and supplication, with thanksgiving, let your requests be made known to God;*

> *and the peace of God, which surpasses all understanding, will guard your hearts and minds through Christ Jesus.*

> Philippians 4:6-7

That's one of those commands with a promise. If we refuse to be anxious about the race and let our requests be made known to

God, then the peace of God will rule our hearts and minds. When we worry, we take charge of our own lives and run our own races to seek our own dreams. Worry is a weight that can lead to many destructive behaviors, the worst one being that we cease to trust and rely on God and take it all on our own backs.

> *Therefore humble yourselves under the mighty hand of God, that He may exalt you in due time,*
>
> *casting all your care upon Him, for He cares for you.*

1 Peter 5:6-7

Worry doubts God's Word, worry does not trust God, and worry makes us physically and mentally sick. It deprives us of peace. It steals our joy. Dump it!

We also need to dump our obsession with the world. This world is not our home! We're just passing through. We need to focus on our eternal home.

> *Do not love the world or the things in the world. If anyone loves the world, the love of the Father is not in him.*
>
> *For all that is in the world – the lust of the flesh, the lust of the eyes, and the pride of life – is not of the Father but is of the world.*
>
> *And the world is passing away, and the lust of it; but he who does the will of God abides forever.*

1 John 2:15-17

For the love of money is a root of all kinds of evil, for which some have strayed from the faith in their greediness, and pierced themselves through with many sorrows.

But you, O man of God, flee these things and pursue righteousness, godliness, faith, love, patience, gentleness.

Fight the good fight of faith, lay hold on eternal life, to which you were also called and have confessed the good confession in the presence of many witnesses.

1 Timothy 6:10-12

To reach our God-given dreams and attain that wonderful future God has planned for us, we must get unlocked from any situation, any person, any sin, and any weight that holds us back. We must hold on to God, hold on to Jesus, hold on to His peace, and hold on to our faith.

But if anything is holding us back, we must *dump it!*

Divine Comfort

Chapter 9

In the day of my trouble I sought the Lord;
My hand was stretched out in the night without ceasing;
My soul refused to be comforted.

I remembered God, and was troubled;
I complained, and my spirit was overwhelmed.

You hold my eyelids open;
I am so troubled I cannot speak.

I have considered the days of old,
The years of ancient times.

I call to remembrance my song in the night;
I meditate within my heart,
And my spirit makes diligent search.

Will the Lord cast off forever?
And will He be favorable no more?

Has His mercy ceased forever?
Has His promise failed forevermore?

Has God forgotten to be gracious?
Has He in anger shut up His tender mercies?

Psalm 77:2-9

In the last chapter, we touched on a weight that very easily besets so many believers today, and that is mental torment. If we are to achieve all God has for us and be everything He gives us the opportunity to be, we must learn how to be comforted by God in this evil, traumatic world we live in.

In Psalm 77, the psalmist Asaph says that his soul refused to be comforted. He lets us know that he was in trouble. His spirit was overwhelmed. He could not sleep. He was so troubled and depressed that he could not speak. He wondered whether God was angry with him or had forgotten him. Anxiety filled his heart and soul, and the worst part of his pain was the thought that God's mercy was no longer his. He felt desperately alone with his suffering and torment.

The Goal of Torment

This psalm seems to be an accurate description of much of the compulsive anxiety and depression that overwhelm individuals in our society today. This may well be the condition in which you find yourself right now. If so, you are by no means alone. The experts say that more than 15 million Americans suffer from depression, making it the most common psychological disorder in the country. Statistics show that one in four women and one in ten men will have one or more episodes of clinical depression at some time in their lives.

And it's not just anxiety and depression. Our nation seems to be full of chronic worriers. Some folk will not only worry when there really is something to worry about, they'll worry when there is nothing to worry about. They'll search the news for something to get worried about, even if it's halfway around the world. A volcano in the Philippines? "Oh, no, that's polluting our air! I can't breathe!" A nuclear accident in Japan? "That's it. We're all going to get cancer now!"

Anxiety, worry, fear, and depression can harm us in many ways. Not only do they damage our mental health, but they damage our physical bodies and severely hinder our faith in God to perform the impossible. These mental and emotional torments can affect and sometimes cause a host of diseases. Medical research has connected heart trouble, high blood pressure, asthma, and other ailments to worry and anxiety. Various scientific studies have shown a direct link between anxiety and illness. The more anxious and worried a person is, the more likely they are to become ill and the longer the illness will last.

Obviously, these disturbed emotional states can hinder us, and the devil knows this. He knows we can't focus clearly on what God has called us to do today when our emotions are upset and our mind is racing. Our professional involvements, relationships, and inner peace all may be sacrificed on the altar of compulsive anxiety and depression. Life itself can be shortened and its quality reduced by worry and fear. Jesus speaks of men's hearts failing them from fear in Luke 21:26.

I suppose, since I live in Los Angeles, that I could worry myself silly over the possibilities of every earthquake, mud slide, and wildfire that happens here. But the odds are higher that the worry would kill me before any disaster would! Many people, however, allow the worries, the pains, and the outrages of life to wear them down and eventually take them out of their race. And that is what Satan and his cohorts are working toward and counting on when they hammer us with evil thoughts. Not only will we fail to achieve our dreams, but our souls cannot be comforted. Some believers even reach the point of giving up.

Life Is Precious

One of the strongest human drives is the survival instinct residing within all of us. Most people are glad they were born and want to live as long as they can. Life is the most valuable commodity in the universe. Without it, everything else is worthless. We would give up almost any earthly thing to save our lives. When confronted by the robber who says, "Your money or your life," we'd readily give them our wallet to save our lives.

It is a sad truth, however, that some people do not place a high value on their own lives. They are very skeptical and pessimistic regarding the "gift" of life and consider it a terrible experience. They're tired of living but scared of dying, so from time to time they go through a phase of hating every moment of their lives. These periods of depression are usually associated with sorrowful, painful, or unpleasant circumstances which they experience.

In the book of Job, during a raging storm of economic tragedy, bereavement over the death of his children, sickness, emotional abuse, and marital problems, Job spoke some of the most hopeless and negative words I have ever read:

> *After this Job opened his mouth and cursed the day of his birth.*

> *And Job spoke, and said:*

"May the day perish on which I was born,
And the night in which it was said,
'A male child is conceived.' . . .

Why did I not die at birth?
Why did I not perish when I came from the womb?

Why did the knees receive me?
Or why the breasts, that I should nurse?

For now I would have lain still and been quiet,
I would have been asleep;
Then I would have been at rest. . . .

Or why was I not hidden like a stillborn child,
Like infants who never saw light? . . .

Who long for death, but it does not come,
And search for it more than hidden treasures?"

Job 3:1-3,11-13,16,21

There are many people who, like Job, are not enjoying life. Sickness, financial problems, dysfunctional relationships, isolation and loneliness, discontent and lack of self-esteem because of physical characteristics, painful things that people have done to them, the death of loved ones, and a host of other problems cause them to despair of life. Some go so far as to end their lives, to commit suicide. They jump off buildings and bridges, they take poison or pills, they shoot themselves with guns, or they slash their wrists. Sadly, these attempts at suicide seem to peak at the ages of eighteen to twenty-four, when life should hold the greatest promise of adventure and excitement.

From Jesus' words and actions, we cannot doubt that God abhors death and does everything He can to prevent it, defeat it, and even reverse it.

But not all suicide attempts are so overt. There are many people who, in despair, have limited and restricted their lives in other ways. There are many forms of suicide:

Abusing alcohol and drugs.

Functioning far beneath one's potential.

Isolating oneself from people and their needs.

Tuning out emotionally and giving up hope for happiness.

Failing to take care of one's health and safety.

Underestimating and undervaluing oneself, having low self-esteem.

Never seeking or never pursuing one's God-given dream.

However, because of all the evil and tragedy one can experience in this world, I am inclined to ask, "Is life worth living?"

The story is told of the baby bird who, when he hatched from the egg, looked around and then reached up, pulled the cracked shell of the egg back together, and tucked his head back in, saying, "I don't want to be born into this world." But no matter what he wanted, that baby bird had been born, and there was no way he could put that egg back together. To those who are saying, "I wish I had never been born," let me say that there is nothing you can do about it. It does no good to wish you hadn't been born, and there is plenty you can do to make the best of it—I don't care where you came from, what you've done, or what you've been through.

Life is sacred because it is a gift from God. God is the only one who gives it, and He forbids us from taking it away. It doesn't matter that abortion is legal and euthanasia may be soon legalized; they are sins. Why is taking a human life so significant to God? According to Genesis 1:26, mankind is created in God's image. Murdering a human being, therefore, is a serious crime and must be punished. One of the Ten Commandments states, **"You shall not murder"** (Exodus 20:13). In the New Testament, Jesus expanded the Old Testament commandment by giving it a spiritual dimension. "Whoever harbors anger and hatred against his brother without a cause," He said, "is in danger of God's judgment." (See Matthew 5:22.)

For Christians, just being angry or hating someone is unacceptable—and hating yourself and your life applies here. Why? Because life is sacred to God and even words and thoughts of death and destruction toward another human being are repugnant to Him. Remember, He is concerned first and foremost with the condition of the heart, because out of the heart come all the issues of our lives. (See Proverbs 4:23.)

Jesus made the statement that if you see Him, you see the Father. (See John 14:9.) Therefore, whatever He said and did during the time He was on this earth portrayed an exact image of the character, thinking, attitudes, and behavior of God. From Jesus' words and actions, we cannot doubt that God abhors death and does everything He can to prevent it, defeat it, and even reverse it.

When Jesus walked the earth, He brought dead people back to life on many occasions. In Luke 7:11-16 He brought the son of the widow of Nain back to life. In Matthew 9:18-19 and 23-26, He brought the ruler's daughter back to life. In John 11:1-54, He brought Lazarus back to life. And after He died for the sins of the human race, He rose again on the third day so that we might rise again and enjoy eternal, resurrection life. All this more than qualifies Jesus to say,

> *"The thief does not come except to steal, and to kill, and to destroy. I have come that they may have life, and that they may have it more abundantly."*

> John 10:10

Jesus gives us life when He pleads with God the Father on our behalf. He gave us eternal life through His death on the cross, which purchased our pardon. He gives us life when He frees us from the bondage of sin. He gives us life not only in this world but also in the world to come. And since Jesus gives us life, how could we ever think of destroying it?

But There Are Those . . .

There are times when people's souls will refuse to be comforted, and believers are no exception. Those who are needlessly and cruelly wounding and hurting those around them — their souls will refuse to be comforted. I'm talking about the dream killers now. Some people are walking demolition experts. They leave broken hearts, wounded spirits, and devastated lives lying beside every road they have traveled. Their favorite sayings are: "I believe in telling it like it is," and "Forget folk. I'm going to take care of myself." They're thoroughly practiced in the art of spreading pain with a nasty comment and a smirk, with rolling eyes and a well-timed derisive laugh.

Some dream killers are more subtle and try to hide their destruction with a false front of caring. They'll smile and pretend to be concerned as others pour out their problems, but they're really gathering ammunition for their next attack. They love to hear prayer requests because there's always some juicy gossip in there, and they take great pride in making it sound even worse when they tell it to the next person than it was related to them. They're experts in manipulation—they love things and use people instead of loving people and using things. Like jackals and other scavengers, they prefer to attack those who are weak and wounded.

I see this so much in the Church that it tears at my heart. Why can't we build ourselves up and encourage ourselves in the Lord without tearing others down? Those who intentionally harm others will not be comforted because their souls allow them to wreak havoc without conscience. How does someone come to this horrid state of existence? When any of us have hatred, jealousy, or unforgiveness in our heart for people in general or someone in particular, our souls will refuse to be comforted.

> *He who says he is in the light, and hates his brother, is in darkness until now.*
>
> 1 John 2:9

Unforgiveness brings resentment, revenge, and retribution. That's the hard core of some folks' sad little lives. They live to remember every wrong. They nurse them and rehearse them until they're eaten up with anger, resentment, and bitterness. Max Lucado, in his book, *The Applause of Heaven*, says,

Resentment is when you let your hurt become hate. Resentment is when you allow what is eating you to eat you up. Resentment is when you poke, stoke, feed, and fan the fire, stirring the flames and reliving the pain.[1]

It's certainly tempting to go along with our lowest level of human nature and hold on to the resentment, warming ourselves by the fire of our well-justified anger. Of course we'll forgive the people who did us wrong someday, but now we have revenge to plan. We replace peaceful nights of uninterrupted sleep with marathon sessions of tossing, turning, and plotting. We substitute productive hours of work with passionate gossip sessions or even expensive legal appointments. We lose the focus on our spiritual life and our God-given dreams and lock in on what we want to do to the person who has become our enemy.

Even worse than being proactively vengeful in our resentment and bitterness, we can also turn our anger and unforgivenss inward, having pity parties which become longer and more excessive until we think and feel our way to the depths of depression and despair. Essentially we are slowly destroying our heart and soul, sacrificing ourselves on the altar of unforgiveness.

The very emotions themselves are unpleasant and harmful. They are obsessive, compulsive, and pervasive. They overwhelm every good and life-giving thought that might try to occupy the mind. They block the healthy processes that normally character-ize the operation of our bodies. Unforgiveness fills our lives, our

---

[1] Max Lucado, *The Applause of Heaven* (Nashville: Word Publishing, 1999), p. 111.

thoughts, and our conversations with negative things. We can have no peace while it resides in us.

We must turn away from hate and unforgiveness. The demonic deception has us thinking that we are doing harm to the person or persons who harmed us. What a lie! In actual fact, unforgiveness harms us more than anyone else. Booker T. Washington, who rose from slavery to become a great educator, said, "I will permit no man to narrow and degrade my soul by making me hate him."

Incredibly simple yet far-reaching, a purposeful act of forgiveness is the only option that makes sense to someone who wants to achieve their God-given dreams. As long as we hold onto anger and unforgiveness, we ourselves cannot be forgiven. Here is one of the more powerful and life-changing verses of Scripture in the Bible:

> *"For if you forgive men their trespasses, your heavenly Father will also forgive you."*

> Matthew 6:14

If we walk in unforgiveness toward anyone, no matter what they have done to us, we cannot obtain forgiveness from the Father for our own sins. Therefore, as long as we hold on to anger and unforgiveness, we can't reach our dreams. Only by choosing to forgive and throwing off the burden of bitterness, anger, self-pity, and revenge onto the Lord do we restore control of our lives to His loving care. We take anger out of the driver's seat and put our dreams back in.

When we move away from God,
it's only a matter of time
before our house of cards
starts falling down around
us and our glamorous
glass houses shatter into
a million tormenting pieces.

There is another sure way our souls can refuse to be comforted. If we are selfish, covetous, self-centered, and tight of fist and heart, our souls will not be comforted by God. I'm talking now about people who get all they can, and "can" all they get. These are folk who seldom go out of their way to help anybody unless there is something in it for them, folk who don't give anything to the poor or to the church except a hard time and a mocking comment.

If God has blessed us so richly, we should bless others. Jesus said, "**Freely you have received, freely give**" (Matthew 10:8). God's Word makes it clear that a generous, giving heart is essential to walking with Him and thus achieving His plan for our lives.

> *There is one who scatters, yet increases more;*
> *And there is one who withholds more than is right,*
> *But it leads to poverty.*
>
> *The generous soul will be made rich,*
> *And he who waters will also be watered himself.*

Proverbs 11:24-25

God commands us to give the tithe, a tenth portion of all He has given us, to the church for His work, and especially for His less fortunate children. He considered the tithe holy. Malachi 3:10 gives God's opinion of those who refuse to honor Him with their tithes—He calls them robbers and declares the bounty of heaven will be shut to them. It's not surprising at all that the souls of those who do not give should refuse to be comforted. Our God is a giving God, far more generous than we can even imagine, and He cannot abide with a stingy, self-centered, tight-fisted soul.

When we are walking fully in a correct relationship with God, we are in our natural element, like a fish in water. When we're separated from God, we're like a fish out of water, and we would do well to refuse to be comforted. Away from the warmth and wisdom of His presence, we become restless and agitated. Nothing satisfies and peace evades us. God uses this state to bring us back to His presence, just as He did when He first saved us.

God Uses Discomfort

If someone is unsaved, their soul will absolutely refuse to be comforted. They have no assurance of life in the world to come, no hope of help in this present world, no benevolent power committed to them, and no sense of a divine companion being in charge of and responsible for their well-being. They walk the earth like a high-wire artist without a net, always one wrong step away from disaster. The Bible says that **the wicked are like the troubled sea,/When it cannot rest,/Whose waters cast up mire and dirt** (Isaiah 57:20). It says that **the wicked flee when no one pursues** (Proverbs 28:1).

Some whose souls refuse to be comforted will do everything but the right thing to find comfort and relief. They will try to ignore the discomfort of their souls. They will try to feed their souls the material things of the world and obtain satisfaction and security, but no matter how much stuff they get, they are still empty and bored to the bone. A very rich but jaded man put it this way:

The eye is not satisfied with seeing,
Nor the ear filled with hearing.

That which has been is what will be,
That which is done is what will be done,
And there is nothing new under the sun.

Ecclesiastes 1:8-9

"Been there, done that. What's next?" Sated with every toy and experience, their souls will say, "This does not satisfy, and I'm still not happy." Seeking satisfaction from every source but the right source, they will exhaust their bodies to give their souls merriment and revelry, parties and games. We see it every day in people who have to go out to clubs where the music is loud and the light is low. They go looking for love in all the wrong places and find only loneliness and more torment. Finally, in that inevitable quiet moment, their souls will tell them, "You're wrong. I'm still not happy."

They lavish sinful, sexual pleasures on themselves, seeking heterosexual, homosexual, bisexual, and even trisexual experiences — they'll try anything. They become addicted to the use of pornography to quiet their raging needs, but it's never enough. No matter what they try or with whom they try it, still their souls will remind them, "You're still wrong, because **the wages of sin is death, but the gift of God is eternal life"** (Romans 6:23).

Some folk would never consider sexual sin, but they get their pleasure, their brief comfort, from indulging themselves in all matter of food. How could eating be sin since we have to eat to live? But food has become their idol, their friend, their refuge in times of trouble. They eat to celebrate, they eat to console

Everything we have
or will be starts
out as potential.

themselves, but deep in their hearts they know that they cannot comfort their souls by feeding their bellies.

Seeking an escape from the conviction in their souls, many try to drug and drink their conscience into silence. It may start as an occasional binge to anesthetize themselves from a momentary pain. But then they need it more and more to stop the hurting. They say, "Maybe if I stay drunk or high, I won't be so unhappy and troubled." But even drunk, their souls stagger up and say, "You're wrong. I'm still unhappy, I still refuse to be comforted, and now you've lost your family and your job."

Most preachers can tell of times when individuals have entered the sanctuary strongly under the influence of drugs or alcohol. It's a wonderful sight because the Holy Spirit has drawn them, even in their state, to a place where their souls can indeed be comforted. But so often those individuals, instead of giving in to the overwhelming love of God, tear themselves away from their moment of redemption and hurl themselves back into their pain rather than be comforted. It breaks my heart every time I see it.

The most heartbreaking sight, however, is that of a believer who has chosen to leave the ways and presence of God to do their own thing, to taste the supposed delights of this world. I wish they had read the book of Ecclesiastes before they decided to do this! It was written by the wisest man in the world, King Solomon, who also was King David and Bathsheba's son. He was a believer who left fellowship with the Lord to pursue every natural pleasure the world offered. The Bible tells us just how low Solomon sunk before he turned back to the Lord:

But King Solomon loved many foreign women, as well as the daughter of Pharaoh: women of the Moabites, Ammonites, Edomites, Sidonians, and Hittites –

from the nations of whom the LORD had said to the children of Israel, "You shall not intermarry with them, nor they with you. Surely they will turn away your hearts after their gods." Solomon clung to these in love.

And he had seven hundred wives, princesses, and three hundred concubines; and his wives turned away his heart.

For it was so, when Solomon was old, that his wives turned his heart after other gods; and his heart was not loyal to the LORD his God, as was the heart of his father David.

For Solomon went after Ashtoreth the goddess of the Sidonians, and after Milcom the abomination of the Ammonites.

Solomon did evil in the sight of the LORD, and did not fully follow the LORD, as did his father David.

Then Solomon built a high place for Chemosh the abomination of Moab, on the hill that is east of Jerusalem, and for Molech the abomination of the people of Ammon.

And he did likewise for all his foreign wives, who burned incense and sacrificed to their gods.

1 Kings 11:1-8

Not only did he marry and take as concubines hundreds of women who were idol worshippers, Solomon also worshipped their gods and even built altars upon which they could sacrifice to their gods. At the end of it all he exclaimed,

Remember your Creator before the silver cord is loosed,
Or the golden bowl is broken,
Or the pitcher shattered at the fountain,
Or the wheel broken at the well. . . .

Let us hear the conclusion of the whole matter:
Fear God and keep His commandments,
For this is man's all.

For God will bring every work into judgment,
Including every secret thing,
Whether good or evil.

Ecclesiastes 12:6,13-14

If anyone had the money and the brains to get everything he could out of life apart from God, it was Solomon. Yet he ultimately came to the conclusion that everything mankind strives to accomplish without God will come to waste and destruction. When we move away from God, it's only a matter of time before our house of cards starts falling down around us and our glamorous glass houses shatter into a million tormenting pieces.

Some folk are in absolutely dire straits because they have fled as far as they can get from God and His ways. The question is, how much misery can they take before they admit their sin and return to Him? How far down do they have to get before they look up? I only hope they won't get as bad as the people of Israel, who were starving in their cities and surrounded by drought and famine because they continued to worship idols rather than the one true God. (See Amos 4:6-13.)

How bad does it have to get before we turn to God? Many lost people die in the depths of their sin, having delayed their return too long. If I were teetering on the brink of hell, my soul could not be comforted either! I would not sleep for fear of waking up in the agonizing torment of hell. Yet in His amazing mercy, God is not willing to give up on those who are still in sin. He waits with undying hope for them to turn from their errant ways. When at last they turn, He welcomes them into the kingdom with open arms. Jesus invites everyone, no matter how low they have sunk, to come:

> *"Come to Me, all you who labor and are heavy laden, and I will give you rest.*
>
> *"Take My yoke upon you and learn from Me, for I am gentle and lowly in heart, and you will find rest for your souls.*
>
> *"For My yoke is easy and My burden is light."*
>
> Matthew 11:28-30

God gives no comfort to the unbeliever and the believer who has strayed except to prove Himself to them and lead them into His kingdom. Then once they commit themselves to Jesus and make Him the Lord of their lives, He bathes them in the comfort and peace of the Holy Spirit. Chuck Colson says of his conversion to Christ,

> I sat there for a long time in that driveway thinking about my life, thinking about what he had told me about Jesus and wanting more than anything else in the world to know God and be at peace with Him. I cried out that

night, I'm not even sure of the words, "Just take me,
God. Take me the way I am." I sat in that car for a long
time that evening and the next morning I was sure when
I woke up I would feel embarrassed. I didn't. I felt a
wonderful, wonderful sense of peace.[2]

Chuck Colson was one of the best-educated, most powerful
men in the United States at one time, but he was lost and empty
and his soul would not be comforted until he came to Jesus.
Whether our lives are good or bad, we can't clean ourselves up
enough to come before God, so it's pointless to try. The cleanest,
sleekest, best-dressed individuals are still stained with sin until
the blood of Jesus is applied to their heart.

If you've never accepted Jesus Christ as your Lord and
Savior, or if you are a child of God who has either wandered
away or run away from the One who cares about you more than
anyone else does, don't wait another moment and don't try to
clean up your life by yourself. Just come home! Let Jesus comfort
your soul right now.

How to Be Comforted

Worry and fear, like pain, can be good if they alert us to our
sick spiritual condition and motivate us to do the right thing
and get right with God. But when there's no good reason for

---

[2] Chuck Colson. "Chuck Colson: Thank God for Watergate, Part Two." Life
Stories: Autobiographies Worth Listening To. Website. (Sumas, WA: Life Story
Foundation. Accessed: 25 August 2000.). *http://www.lifestory.org/cols2.html*

torment and we are truly living for God, these emotions are out of place. Sometimes when our souls refuse to be comforted, they *should* be comforted.

Sometimes there is no real reason for worry, but still we are worried. Sometimes God is doing everything in our lives that He should, but we're still upset and disturbed. Sometimes everything is all right, yet we feel that things are all wrong. For example, when we are saved but don't feel saved, our souls should be comforted. Salvation is not a matter of feeling. The blood of Jesus doesn't get the blues or get happy. It never changes. What happens is that we allow Satan to whisper accusations in our ears and we fall for his lies. When we start to believe we might not be saved, then we begin to feel a little unsaved, and the downward spiral continues until hopelessness fills our being.

This is where the renewing of our mind is so vital and essential to a Christian's well-being. There is no way we can ever pursue and achieve our dreams without a renewed mind because the enemy will talk us out of righteousness, peace, and joy every time. Therefore, as soon as we have that first thought that we might not be saved, we should meditate on this scripture and allow the truth of it to penetrate our souls:

But God, who is rich in mercy, because of His great love with which He loved us,

even when we were dead in trespasses, made us alive together with Christ (by grace you have been saved),

and raised us up together, and made us sit together in the heavenly places in Christ Jesus,

that in the ages to come He might show the exceeding
riches of His grace in His kindness toward us in Christ Jesus.

For by grace you have been saved through faith, and that
not of yourselves; it is the gift of God,

not of works, lest anyone should boast.

Ephesians 2:4-9

Once the truth of that Word really hits us, we should not only be comforted but shouting from the rooftops! We've been made alive with Christ Jesus! We are not dead in our sins! Hallelujah!

When you have repented and asked God for forgiveness but don't feel forgiven, your soul should be comforted because if you confess your sins, He is faithful and just to forgive you your sins and to cleanse you from all unrighteousness. (See 1 John 1:9.) That verse is God's truth no matter how we feel. Don't listen to the devil, the accuser of the brethren. (See Revelation 12:10.) He's lying because he can't stand to see us walking with God and pursuing our dreams.

Even when we endure difficult trials and hardships, our soul should be comforted. Did you know that the Christians in China — forced underground by decades of severe oppression — pray that American believers will undergo religious persecution as they do? They pray for us to be persecuted so we might be as blessed as they are. They're not blessed with material things; they're blessed with an incredibly strong faith and a close walk with the Lord. In fact, in some areas they are under such persecution that they cannot announce the time and place of their meetings for fear of being arrested. They simply pray, and the Holy Spirit tells them when and where to gather for worship. They see our faith and Christian walk as weak and unstable, and they pray that we'll be blessed with persecution that strengthens us.

> *My brethren, count it all joy when you fall into various trials,*
>
> *knowing that the testing of your faith produces patience.*
>
> *But let patience have its perfect work, that you may be perfect and complete, lacking nothing.*

James 1:2-4

Our souls should also be comforted when our resources are low. God didn't let Gideon fight the Midianites until he was impossibly low on manpower. Jesus didn't feed the crowds until it was humanly impossible. God does not start to supply until we don't have enough. That way, when we do succeed, He gets the glory and not us. When our resources are down to nothing, we are in just the right condition for God to move, and He's never too early or too late. When we are pursuing the dream He has given us, and we have faith in His provision, our "not enough" becomes His "more than enough."

Furthermore, our souls should be comforted when we have come to a dead end. As Pharaoh's army charged toward them, Moses and the children of Israel came to a dead end against the shore of the Red Sea, but the Lord forged a highway through the sea. When we are going the way He tells us to go, He will make sure the path is clear. We just have to walk by faith, not by sight. (See 2 Corinthians 5:7.) We don't focus on the sea in front or the army behind, but on the promise of God, the dream He dropped into our hearts.

Even when it's time for us to die, our souls should be comforted. We are confident that to be absent from the body is to be present with the Lord. (See 2 Corinthians 5:8.) Death should hold no terror for the believer, only comfort and anticipation of the reunion to come.

"Well Preacher, I've heard what you have said, but what do I do when my soul refuses to be comforted, even when it should?" Let's examine what the psalmist did. Psalm 77:1 says that he cried out to God. He prayed. That is a good strategy because we're promised that if we pray, the peace of God will guard our hearts.

> *Be anxious for nothing, but in everything by prayer and supplication, with thanksgiving, let your requests be made known to God;*
>
> *and the peace of God, which surpasses all understanding, will guard your hearts and minds through Christ Jesus.*
>
> Philippians 4:6

Prayer is a two-way conversation. Too many times we tell God everything but never let Him get a word in edgewise. The truth is, He has much to say!

> *"'Call to Me, and I will answer you, and show you great and mighty things, which you do not know.'"*
>
> Jeremiah 33:3

For God to answer and show us His plan for our lives, much less **great and mighty things,** we need to shut up and listen to

Him. He knows everything we know, and we don't know a fraction of what He knows, so why are we doing all the talking when we pray?

In Psalm 77:2, the psalmist says he sought *the Lord.* Notice he does not say he sought *the Lord's blessings.* When we stop going after *His,* and start going after *Him,* our souls will be comforted. When we seek His face rather than His hand, when we say, "Lord, I want *You* more that I want Your blessings," God will give us Himself, our souls will be comforted, and then His blessings will overtake us.

How else can we be comforted? Rather than mulling over past failures, we can count our blessings and remember all the wonderful things God has done for us. Even if we have just accepted the Lord, we can look back and see how He has drawn us to Himself through the years. In Psalm 77:11, the psalmist said,

> *I will remember the works of the LORD;*
> *Surely I will remember Your wonders of old.*

Remembering the grace and mercy of the Lord brings His divine comfort into our hearts. No matter how physically able we are, we can relive the memories of the day we were saved, the day we saw a loved one healed, all the times God has answered prayer. And then the psalmist said:

> *I will also meditate on all Your work,*
> *And talk of Your deeds.*

Psalm 77:12

Not only should we remember, but we should reminisce at length and tell others. We should sit our children and grandchildren at our knee and tell of the glories of the Lord. Many an adult has returned to the Lord after remembering the Bible stories their mother or father, grandmother or grandfather, or even a great aunt or uncle told them as a child.

There is a principle in the kingdom of God which seems very ironic, but like all God's principles, it works. This is how it works: God saves us and then we bring others to salvation. God loves us and then we can love others. God forgives us and then we can forgive others. God prospers us and then we can prosper others. And when we receive comfort from the Lord, we are obligated to give the same comfort to those who are going through the same trial or any trial. Trouble is trouble and God wants to comfort all of His children. The apostle Paul put it this way:

> *Blessed be the God and Father of our Lord Jesus Christ, the Father of mercies and God of all comfort,*
>
> *who comforts us in all our tribulation, that we may be able to comfort those who are in any trouble, with the comfort with which we ourselves are comforted by God.*

> 2 Corinthians 1:3-4

One of the reasons Alcoholics Anonymous, Weight Watchers, and other support-group organizations are so successful is because they operate according to this principle. When a person shares the comfort they have received with another person who is going through a trial, both of them are comforted. Comfort is multiplied and people are set free. Do you see how powerful and vital it is for our souls to be comforted?

We must continuously be receiving divine comfort to walk in peace, achieve our dreams, and help others to achieve theirs. In order to walk in this way, however, we must meditate on the things of God rather than the things of earth. If we consistently and steadfastly continue in these things, our souls will be comforted. We can't just do these things occasionally and then complain they don't work. We have to be consistent in our efforts, and then they will work. That would be like going on a diet each day for ten minutes and eating everything in sight the rest of the time. That won't work! We can't expect our souls to be comforted without effort on our part, just as we can't expect to reach our dreams without effort. God is faithful to do His part, but we must do ours.

Divine Potential

When we are functioning and living up to our potential, our souls shall be comforted. God has deposited within each of us a great store of potential. He desires to use that potential to enhance our lives, the lives of those around us, and to bring glory to His name. He gives us these gifts, talents, and abilities to achieve the dreams and plans He has placed in our hearts. The poet Carl Sandburg said, "Nothing happens unless first a dream." Everything we have or will be starts out as *potential.*

It doesn't matter if we can't immediately see the potential God has invested in us. Great people are never great initially. They only have the potential for greatness. Achievement requires effort. Genius Thomas Edison said, "Invention is 1 percent inspiration and 99 percent perspiration." Joseph didn't look like he had much potential when he was tossed into the pit, and things didn't look much better when he was in prison for years. *If God has given you a dream to do something, trust Him that He has stored in you the potential to accomplish that dream.*

But when we fail to reach that dream, we waste the potential God has invested in us. And when we waste what God has given, our souls refuse to be comforted.

Life is a matter of degrees. Some people have more life than others because they have developed their potential more than others. Jesus said that He came to give us abundant life, and that means that when we are born again, He deposits in us the divine potential for abundant life. When we stir up our gifts, operate in them, follow His Word, and obey the Holy Spirit's every direction, we will see the powerful manifestation of abundant life.

When a sick man is healed, he has life more abundantly than he did when he was sick.

When a prisoner is set free, he has life more abundantly than he did when he was in prison.

When a poor man becomes rich, he has life more abundantly than he did when he was poor.

When a man who was totally alone finds a family and friends, he has life more abundantly than he did when he was alone.

If our lives are less than others or less than we would like, it's simply because we need more of Jesus. Pursuing Jesus ignites the divine potential for abundance within us.

Jesus gives abundant life because He makes us whole and complete.

Jesus gives abundant life because He gives us freedom.

Jesus gives abundant life because He gives us exceeding great joy.

Jesus gives us abundant life because He gives eternal life now.

Jesus gives us abundant life because He uses all the gifts, talents, and abilities He has placed in us to bring our God-given dreams to pass.

When we fully realize the treasure we have in our *abundant* life in Christ and comprehend the scope of our eternal life in Him, thoughts of ending or minimizing our present existence should fade away like the morning fog. When we truly commit to the unrelenting pursuit of our God-given dreams, our soul is comforted and we can't wait to see what tomorrow holds.

The Only Reason *to* Dream

Chapter 10

Tommy was eight, the middle boy of six children. Money was tight in his family, but there was always plenty of love. Now one of Tommy's regular chores was to polish his Sunday shoes on Saturday night. It was one chore he never had to be reminded to do because he really enjoyed the whole process — the smell of the wax, the ritual of applying the polish, then buffing the shoes till they glowed.

This one Saturday night, his dad was having to work late and his mom was busy with the million and one things that moms do. So Tommy up and decided to polish his parents' Sunday shoes. He carefully took his dad's black wingtips and polished them, just the way he'd seen his dad do it. Then he carefully cleaned and polished his mom's good black pumps. When he was done, he put them back in their places without saying a word.

Dad noticed, and Sunday morning, right before church, he pulled Tommy aside and thanked him for his thoughtfulness. He told Tommy that his shoes had never looked better. Then he slipped Tommy a shiny quarter, which was quite a precious item in those days. After church, Tommy seemed unusually quiet, and then just before sitting down to dinner, Tommy approached his dad. With a tear on his cheek, he slipped the quarter back into his dad's hand and said, "Daddy, I didn't do it for the money. I done it for love."

We can seek to achieve our God-given dreams for many reasons, but the only valid one is love. It is only out of our love for God that we should pursue the dreams that He blesses us with. We shouldn't pursue them for our own sakes or for the sake of our family or for our church. God put us here for His glory, and we are to pursue His plan for no other reason than to glorify Him. If we approach the process with any other motivation, we'll fail. And we'll probably blame Him for our failure!

Courage and Persistence

As we look at the nuts and bolts of pursuing our God-given dreams, we can easily recognize that only when we do something for the right reason will everything else fall into place. It is only a committed love for God that will motivate us and sustain us when we go through the ups and downs of fulfilling the dreams He has given us.

There are two vital components in the formula for godly success which are rooted in our love for God. First, we need courage, and I'm not sure we all understand what courage really is. It can be a fearful thing to stick our necks out and go after our dreams. Without courage, we'll never do it. Several times in Joseph's rise from the pit to the palace, he had to courageously do the right thing despite the consequences. He never would have reached his dream without bravery. Courage backed his every step.

But how does courage help us? "Courage," observed Samuel Johnson, "is the greatest of all the virtues, because if you haven't courage, you may not have an opportunity to use any of the others." When we have courage, we'll be able to see ourselves as God sees us, admit that we're dissatisfied with our own plan for our lives, and decide to do something about it. With courage, we can grab the opportunities that lead to our God-given dreams.

Now that's not to say that we're not scared too, even as we're pursuing our dreams. Sure, there will often be apprehension. Can you have fear and courage at the same time? Aren't they opposites? Isn't being scared the opposite of being brave? Consider this: Kids are well acquainted with being scared — they get frightened about all kinds of things. Usually it's the fear of doing something new or going somewhere new that's so scary to them. Remember how, as a child, the first time you rode a bike, or the first time you went to school? Now that was scary. You didn't know how, and you were afraid that you'd get hurt or make a fool of yourself. But eventually we all rode that bike and went to school *because we had enough courage to overcome our fear.* That's right — we were brave in spite of our fear. There is no need for courage if there is nothing to fear. When we show courage, we master and overcome fear. Courage is merely a tool we use to overcome the fear that keeps us from reaching for our dreams.

Believers can show tremendous courage when they are walking in the love of God. They have no doubt that whatever God calls them to do, He will be there to provide for them and

There is no need for courage if there is nothing to fear.

protect them. There's no question that even if they misunderstand and mess up, God will be there to help them up when they fall. He knows we're human and we're bound to fail once in awhile! That's the price of daring to dream. I like what President Teddy Roosevelt said: "Far better it is to dare mighty things, to win glorious triumphs, even though checkered by failure, than to rank with those poor spirits who neither enjoy much nor suffer much because they live in the gray twilight that knows neither victory nor defeat."

In addition to courage, reaching our God-given dreams requires persistence. Persistence is a peculiar trait that acts together with other traits to multiply their effectiveness. Persistence adds leverage to any force we apply. Consider this famous quote from President Calvin Coolidge: "Nothing in the world can take the place of persistence. Talent will not; the world is full of unsuccessful men with talent. Genius will not; unrewarded genius is almost a proverb. Education will not; the world is full of educated derelicts. Persistence and determination alone are omnipotent."

Think about that. Coolidge said that reaching our dreams takes talent *plus* persistence, genius *plus* persistence, education *plus* persistence. But what if we're not particularly talented, educated, or smart? Well, that's still not an insurmountable problem. Even without talent, genius, or education, sheer dogged persistence will take us farther than anything else.

In my life, I've seen that persistence is closely linked to motivation. When we're motivated strongly enough, we will persist, and nothing motivates like love. Would most men swim a shark-infested bay, cross a burning desert, then climb a sheer cliff just to visit their mother-in-law? Probably not. But what if they were trying to save the life of their child? Would that not motivate them to make the same trip and to keep on trying no matter what? Wouldn't they overcome every obstacle, try any alternative, make any effort required to accomplish their task? If we make seeking God's plan for our lives then pursuing that dream until it is accomplished a high enough priority — a matter of loving Him — we will be motivated to persist in our efforts no matter what happens along the way.

Persistence, then, is more like the deliberate, thoughtful, sequential search for all possible alternative routes on our way to our goals. It's not the fly banging against a window in futile repeated attempts to do something impossible. Persistence is more like an ant at a picnic, seeking a way to get to the fried chicken. And they always get there!

Why Don't We Dream?

When we were born, God placed dreams in our hearts, but for many of us, somewhere along the way we stopped dreaming. Maybe we saw our father or aunt step out in faith to pursue a dream that was foolishness and not from God. Of course, they fell flat on their face and we were ashamed, embarrassed, and yet terribly relieved it was them and not us. Maybe we saw someone step out in faith for a God-given dream, come up against persecution and affliction, and quit or even die. But the most common reason we refuse to dream is because we consider dreaming wonderful dreams to be kid stuff. Nothing could be further from the truth!

We start dreaming when we're young, of course. Kids naturally dream of doing great things. A little boy might want to be the starting quarterback for the Dallas Cowboys one day, a missionary to China the next day, and an astronaut a week later. A little girl may want to be an Olympic champion on Monday, Miss America on Wednesday, and go to Africa to feed the hungry on Sunday. Adults have not yet convinced children that they can't do all of those things.

Eventually, however, those dreams turn into memories. Most kids are taught to put away those silly dreams as they grow up. Their folk tell them, "Be a doer, not a dreamer." Teachers caution them, "You're gonna sit there and daydream your life away and won't amount to anything." When they're teenagers, their friends laugh at them when they mention any high aspiration, even if they have the same dream. It isn't long before they learn that little kids dream, but grown-ups don't. Most parents consider it a sign of maturity when their children begin to give up on silly childhood dreams. We're pleased when we see them facing up to reality and "getting a grip on real life." We even quote the Bible at them, saying,

> *When I was a child, I spoke as a child . . . but when I became a man, I put away childish things.*

> 1 Corinthians 13:11

Dreams are not childish! But ultimately, we force our children to choose between their dreams and what we insist is reality. All too soon they're in what we call "the real world," like us, with their dreams only a fading memory. As we grow up, we follow our role models, family, and friends of the family whom we see on a regular basis. They show us what's normal adult behavior. If no one we know pursues their God-given dreams or even admits to having them, we don't learn the practice either. If we're brought up with the habit of just getting by, of doing the same old things the same old way, that's all we ever learn. We do just enough to survive in school and sports and our part-time job.

We then carry these bad habits into our work lives, our marriages, and into our roles as parents. When we look around and compare our lives with folk around us, we usually don't see enough difference to change our ways. We just assume this is all there is to life. But there's so much more! Our spiritual lives, our families, our marriages, our careers, and our churches could be so much more fulfilling if we'd break those dead habits and pursue the plan God has for our lives.

We only have a problem when we see someone who's really living their dreams. That upsets our little semi-satisfied world! We have to tell ourselves that those folk are successful because they got all the breaks, their families have lots of money, or some other excuse. It would just about kill us to admit that they're just average people who are more successful than we are simply because they chose to dream and to work to make their dreams come true.

Zero In

Whatever has caused us not to dream, how can we dream again? How can we regain that childlike belief that God really does have a wonderful plan for our lives? How can we dump years of unbelief, cynicism, and laziness? By zeroing in on God's love for us and then acting out of that love. If He loved us so much that He sent Jesus to die for us, we should rise up and declare that we're not willing to settle for the devil's leftovers, that we're not going to let life just happen to us. No longer will we see ourselves as victims and blame our parents, our spouses, our bosses, or the government. We will take the steps of faith necessary to achieve our God-given dreams.

George Bernard Shaw once said, "People are always blaming their circumstances for what they are. I don't believe in circumstances. The people who get on in this world are the people who get up and look for the circumstances they want, and if they can't find them, make them."

When we realize God loves us and has a marvelous plan for our lives, we can give ourselves permission to dream again. While adults should not be childish, it's really okay to be child-like and dream of wonderful things. In the beginning, it is wise to keep our decision to ourselves. We shouldn't be advertising the fact that we've decided to dream again because we may still be too fragile to withstand the abuse from dream killers. We simply must decide that discovering our buried dreams is the first step to living God's plan for our lives.

Now, rather than dreaming the way a child does, this time we'll dream with our hearts open to the Holy Spirit. We should ask God what His wildest dream for our lives is. He's waiting for us to ask, and He's wanting to tell us because He loves us. Moreover, He wants to tell us what it is and how to do it.

The act of expressing
our dreams tangibly
in writing also gives
them the power of
our conviction.

If any of you lacks wisdom, let him ask of God, who gives to all liberally and without reproach, and it will be given to him.

James 1:5

It helps to be able to get alone with God for this important time. Unfortunately, solitude is a very rare commodity in our busy lives. We're usually surrounded by people and their noisy demands all day. But we must free our minds and separate ourselves from the tyranny of the urgent so we can relax, pray, and dream. When we believe we've heard from God, it's important to compare what we've heard to the Word of God. If it doesn't line up with the Bible, we've not heard from the Holy Spirit but some other spirit! Remember, God's wonderful plan for our lives will glorify God, not us. His plan will hurt no one, nor will it cause damage to the body of Christ.

Don't worry if the dream God reveals to you makes absolutely no sense in the natural or if it seems so unlikely as to be laughable. That's why reaching for our dreams requires faith. Joseph was the next-to-last son of his father. For him to reach a position where his big brothers would bow to him and pay him homage made no sense and was utterly unlikely. Yet he knew the dream was from God, so he believed it would come to pass. We must not put limits on our God-given dreams. A great big God will not fit into our tiny little box. Our human understanding cannot deal with God's big-picture plan for our lives. We simply have to believe, obey, and know that it will all make sense when we see the dream come true.

As we seek God for His plans for our lives, we need to use a pen and paper to write down what He shows us.

Another thing to watch out for is unbelief masquerading as humility. We must not tell God He can't do great things with us just because we think we're only "poor little us." He knows what we are! That's exactly why He gets the glory, because He uses the least of us to do the greatest things. He's also watching how we handle small amounts of success. If we hog His glory over little things, He's not likely to bless us with more just so we can have an even bigger ego trip. But again, if our motivation is love for Him, His glory will radiate from our faces!

Get It on Paper

When we love God, He will give us a vision and plan for our lives, and when He imparts it to us, He asks us to write the vision down. When we write things down, they become clear and take on a meaning and substance they didn't have before. God knows that there is something solid and unshakeable about the written word!

> *Then the LORD answered me and said:*
> *"Write the vision*
> *And make it plain on tablets,*
> *That he may run who reads it.*
>
> *"For the vision is yet for an appointed time;*
> *But at the end it will speak, and it will not lie.*
> *Though it tarries, wait for it;*
> *Because it will surely come,*
> *It will not tarry.*

Habbakuk 2:2-3

In 1953, researchers polled the graduating class of Yale University and found that only 3 percent of the graduates had a set of clearly defined, written dreams. Twenty years later, researchers went back and surveyed that same class again. The results were astounding. The researchers found that the 3 percent of graduates who had written down their dreams twenty years before had built fortunes worth more than the other 97 percent combined!

As we seek God for His plans for our lives, we need to use a pen and paper to write down what He shows us. It's very important to write them down because when we do, they're not easy to forget and ignore in the rush of everyday life. Once we commit our dreams to paper, they become a solid point to which we can keep referring. The act of expressing our dreams tangibly in writing also gives them the power of our conviction. Tucked in our Bibles or posted where we see them every day, they can be used as a constant reminder of God's love for us and our commitment to living a life lined up with His perfect will.

As we pray over God's ultimate plan for our future, let us also be open to hear His desires for other areas of our lives. Because we love Him, we want to line up with His will in every area of life, not just in His ultimate dream, His wonderful plan. God is concerned with our marriages, our families, our careers, our churches, and everything that concerns us.

We can sit down and come up with a written list of inspired dreams—things that God says we can and should achieve in our lifetimes—for every part of our lives. It's good to use a separate piece of paper for each area of dreams, and we should be as clear and specific as possible. To reinforce our commitment to our dreams, we should selectively share our lists of dreams with those whom we know we can trust. As I said before, some folk will take great pleasure in stomping all over our shiny new dreams. We have to make sure that the people we share our dreams with are godly people who already know God's plan for their lives. We also must know that those we trust with our dreams are not gossips, that they can and will keep our confidence. There's nothing worse than hearing something we said in confidence become a juicy bit of trash among folk we thought were our friends! But there is nothing like the encouragement of a godly friend who understands the process of fulfilling God's call on our lives.

The Moment of Truth

At this point, you have a choice. You can finish this book, put it down, and go on living your life the same way you always have. Rather than living to reach for the stars, you can just live to reach payday. You can put this book aside and give up on your dreams, accepting with a shrug whatever pitiful existence life dishes out to you. Or, you can put what you've learned into action. You can stand up, stomp your foot and say, "Devil, you've taken me for a fool long enough! It's over! I will not settle for less than the very best that God has for me! I love God more than my own life and I will not give up, shut up, lie down, or roll over until I have run as hard as I can after His perfect will for my life!" You can look at your life and declare,

"What is behind me is past *because God loves me.*

"My present circumstances will not hold me back, put me down, or trip me up *because God loves me.*

"I refuse to accept my present life as a limit to my future *because God loves me.*

"Neither hatred, nor pit, nor prison will deter me from reaching my God-given dreams *because God loves me.*

"I have no faith in my circumstances but only in God *because God loves me.*

"My hope is only in the Lord who has a wonderful plan for my life, a plan to prosper me and not to harm me; a dream that will lift me up, not put me down because He loves me!"

Now speak to God in the name of your Savior and Lord, Jesus Christ:

Father, I come to You in Jesus' name to declare my love and commitment to You right now. You know I have followed my own way and chased my own dreams for too much of my life. I have picked out the blessing I wanted and told You to bless me in my selfishness. I have failed to seek Your wisdom, Your guidance, and Your heart. I have run my mouth in prayer rather than listen to Your voice.

Forgive me, Lord God, in the name of Jesus, for these sins. I make a solemn pledge to turn away from them and walk in the ways of righteousness. As I repent of my self-centered life, restore to me the joy of my salvation and reawaken the freshness of new birth in me.

Now I humbly ask You, Lord, to fill my heart with Your dreams for my life. Show me Your plan for my future. Anoint my ears with Your Spirit, Lord, and allow my eyes to see Your vision so that I may rise up

*and transform my world through Your great power and bring glory to
Your name.*

*I step out in faith now, Lord, knowing that You will do exceedingly
abundantly above all I can ask or think. I choose to walk in Your ways
with my eyes fixed firmly on the dreams You have given me. Thank You
for loving me, Father! Amen.*

If you just prayed that prayer with your whole heart and
meant it from the depths of your being, if you are completely
committed to what you have just prayed, then rejoice and be
glad! Kick up your heels and dance for joy! Not only are your
greatest adventures about to begin, but I believe Jesus Christ is
leaping to His feet and crying, "Look Father, they are now FREE
TO DREAM!"

About the Author

Bishop Charles E. Blake Sr. is pastor of West Angeles Church of God in Christ, the largest African American church in the western United States. Bishop Blake has overseen its growth from a 50-member church in 1969 to a membership of over 18,000 at this writing, making it one of the fastest growing congregations in the world. He and his co-chairmen, Magic Johnson and Denzel Washington, are now overseeing a $60 million building project to build West Angeles Cathedral, which is estimated to have an economic impact of $100 million on the community of South Los Angeles. Moreover, the church includes 80-plus specialty ministries that are already making a substantial difference in the city.

Bishop Blake serves as one of the 12-member General Board of the Church of God in Christ, the presiding board of the 2.2 million-member denomination. Since 1985, he has been the Jurisdictional Prelate of the First Jurisdiction of Southern California, which owns and maintains Bonnie Brae House, where the Azuza Revival began, and Transition House, a substance abuse recovery facility for men. As prelate, he oversees approximately 230 churches that make up the First Jurisdiction.

Bishop Blake was the chair of the founding board of directors for C. H. Mason Theological Seminary, and formerly served as member of the executive committee of the board of directors, as well as board member of the board of directors for the Interdenominational Theological Seminary. He is a former chair of the executive committee and member of the board of directors of Oral Roberts University and is a member of the board of directors of Charismatic Bible Ministries.

Currently, Bishop Blake serves as an advisory committee member of the Pentecostal World Conference and is the founder and cochair of the Los Angeles Ecumenical Congress, an interdenominational coalition of religious leaders and pastors dedicated to the reestablishment of African American Christian leadership in the city of Los Angeles. Armed with a spiritual and moral agenda, the LAEC seeks to effectively utilize its collective influence among community and political leadership to benefit Los Angeles residents and respond to the challenges which face the community.

Bishop Blake is a recipient of the Salvation Army's William Booth Award and the Greenlining Institute's Big Heart Award. He is the recipient of the Los Angeles Urban League's Whitney M. Young Award.

Bishop Blake is married to Mae Lawrence Blake. They are the parents of three children and the grandparents of two grandchildren. Bishop Blake is a respected and dynamic preacher, a world-class leader, a visionary, and a beloved friend and mentor to many. He is internationally recognized as one of America's most profound intellectuals and yet an extraordinary man of God.

To contact Bishop Blake, write:

West Angeles Church of God in Christ

3045 S. Crenshaw Boulevard

Los Angeles, California 90016

or visit his website at:

www.westa.org

Additional copies of this book and other book titles
from **ALBURY PUBLISHING** are
available at your local bookstore.

ALBURY PUBLISHING
P. O. Box 470406
Tulsa, Oklahoma 74147-0406

For a complete list of our titles,
visit us at our website:

www.alburypublishing.com

For international and Canadian orders,
please contact:

Access Sales International

2448 East 81st Street
Suite 4900
Tulsa, Oklahoma 74137
Phone 918-523-5590 Fax 918-496-2822